THE GREAT 8 PILLARS

THE
GREAT

8

PILLARS

ROI-DRIVEN MARKETING FOR MANUFACTURING COMPANIES

CHRISTOPHER PEER

with **JOHN DATERS** and **NADINE NOCERO-TYE**

LIONCREST
PUBLISHING

THE GREAT 8 PILLARS
ROI-Driven Marketing for Manufacturing Companies
First Edition

ISBN 978-1-5445-4407-6 *Hardcover*
       978-1-5445-4406-9 *Paperback*
       978-1-5445-4408-3 *Ebook*

CONTENTS

INTRODUCTION

As humans, we all want to do things faster, with less effort. It's why the diet and exercise industry sells billions of dollars' worth of fad products. This book is not about secret marketing tactics or shortcut remedies to improve metrics. The methodologies included in this book are based on building a professional marketing infrastructure that is scalable and predictable. It's about building a well-oiled machine that continually delivers.

For the past twenty-plus years, I have owned and managed a successful marketing agency, driven by a passion for helping manufacturing companies thrive. Why manufacturing? I don't really know. Perhaps it is because my father was the president of a manufacturing company. There's just a feeling that comes over me when I walk the shop floor and see people working on the various stages of production. Perhaps it's the smell of oil or the exhaust of an older tow motor. Maybe it's the sound of industrial machinery as it cuts, bends, and grinds metal. There's just something about the whole process of manufacturing that intrigues me.

When I first started writing this book, people asked me why I was willing to openly share our proprietary processes and methodologies. Why was I giving away the secrets of our success?

I started my company in 2002, and since then, I have tirelessly worked to hone our marketing methodologies to ensure our manufacturing clients get a return on their investment. My goal is to help them avoid the mistakes that so many others have made while helping them to scale faster and more efficiently. Just as they work so hard to bring quality products to life, I feel that it is my job to deliver for them. It's my turn to give back and help our manufacturing community the best I can.

Over the years, I've found that manufacturing companies have a lot in common when it comes to marketing:

- They don't trust agencies to deliver because many have failed.

- They don't like spending money on things that don't work.
- They don't like wasting time on things that don't work.

Winning a manufacturer's business is a feat in and of itself. You must demonstrate that you can be trusted and that you will deliver on your promises. You must overcome their fears and prove that you understand their business and, perhaps more importantly, that you understand their customers and how they make purchasing decisions.

Through my deep relationships with manufacturers, I also recognized that they all lacked the same operational requirements for driving a marketing return on investment. Of the hundreds of clients my company has served, not a single one had an existing marketing strategy documented in writing prior to our working relationship. Most others did not have the basic foundational elements of a marketing program, such as defined goals, correlating key performance indicators, defined buyer personas, or ideal customer profiles. Some of our clients are small businesses securing $10 million in revenues; others are billion-dollar enterprises. After seeing the pain and frustration shared by so many marketing leaders and executives, we decided to do something about it.

This book outlines my years of marketing experience and explains how to structure your marketing operation using proven strategies, methodologies, and tools to deliver a 10X return on marketing investment (ROI). The Great 8 Pillars of ROI-Driven Marketing framework is based on a system that has consistently delivered outstanding results for my clients. Using this system, my clients earn an ROI from their marketing spend, many of them over 10X; one even attained a 27X return on investment. This system drives marketing ROI while reducing marketing output, stopping work on vanity projects, and measuring the outcomes.

For twenty-plus years, my company, SyncShow, honed its methodology, compiled research, and tested, tweaked, and formalized a tried-and-true approach. We assessed exactly what worked and what didn't. We documented our findings and continually refined them. The result is a marketing framework built to deliver a 10X return on investment from marketing spend, and you can do it too.

The Great 8 Pillars of ROI-Driven Marketing offers manufacturing leaders a helping hand in achieving real results and peace of mind from their marketing effort. It is written for those who are stuck in a world of whack-a-mole-style tactical marketing, where more blogs, more videos, more SEO, and more effort are not working to move the needle.

This book is for you if you are a marketing leader or manufacturing executive who is:

- Investing in growth and looking to scale
- Frustrated that your marketing efforts are not producing the desired results
- Sick and tired of wasting time and money on marketing that does not work
- Confused about knowing what to do and when and how to do it
- Burned out from long working hours and continually reinventing the marketing wheel
- Tired of the monotony of developing more, more, and more marketing collateral
- Frustrated by continuous turnover of your marketing team members

This book outlines exactly how you can do it—every step— including how to build marketing strategies, craft value propositions that stand out, establish ROI-driven marketing goals, define key performance indicators, set up reporting, acquire data, and prove that what you do matters.

This is a book for business-to-business (B2B) marketing and executive leaders who are looking to drive increased performance and a measurable return from marketing. It's for marketing and sales leaders who are looking for a proven system for delivering real ROI from marketing. It's for anyone who is sick and tired of wasting money on marketing that does not work and for anyone who wants long-term results. It's not for marketers who are looking for a quick fix. There is no magic bullet in ROI-driven marketing.

You, too, can drive real change and growth at your company, and I will help you drive a 10X return on marketing spend! It won't be easy. It's hard work. But if you follow the process, it will significantly change the way you look at marketing and how you define success.

I am excited to guide you through this process!

/ / /

Throughout this book, I have included "Lesson Learned" sections, where I share with you some of my failures in marketing. These failures helped to reshape my paradigm on marketing and often were the catalyst for change. Every one of them was a valuable lesson learned. I hope you will find them valuable too.

THE WAKE-UP CALL

It was 2010, and one of our clients was a small but fast-growing manufacturing company in the Midwest. The owner, Jeff, was my business partner's cousin. Jeff was a great guy and a revered leader, regarded in his town as a successful entrepreneur. Jeff and his team were good people with a great product.

To kick off the marketing engagement, my business partner and I drove six hours to meet Jeff and his executive team. We were super excited for this opportunity.

Jeff's company was booming. The problem was that the company didn't have a strong online presence. Their brand awareness beyond a hundred-mile radius of their headquarters was nil. Their dream was to sell their product to one of the major automotive companies. For this small company, it was a lofty objective.

Upon launching the marketing program, we enhanced their messaging, developed brand standards, secured marketing collateral, and launched a new website with a strong focus on search engine optimization (SEO).

As their marketing agency, one of our responsibilities was to track website traffic and the companies that were visiting their website. Months went by. Website traffic was increasing and leads were coming in, but nothing significant. About six months later, we noticed something incredible—visitors from General Motors, Ford, and Chrysler had all visited their website in the same week, and they all had visited the same product page! Excited, we immediately called Jeff.

"Jeff, General Motors, Ford, and Chrysler all were on your website last week, and they all visited XYZ product page," we said. "We did some research and found that the people who visited your site were located in these specific cities. If we make some assumptions regarding their work titles, we could call people with those titles in the corporate offices in those cities and hopefully connect." (Note: This was 2010, and we did not yet have sophisticated lead-tracking software.)

Jeff agreed. His sales team made some calls, and about nine months later, they secured a huge contract with one of the automotive giants valued at over $30 million. We were so excited to have helped drive such tremendous value. We thought Jeff's company would be indebted to us forever. Clients for life! However, we were a bit arrogant, ignorant, and immature in our thinking.

About a year after the big win, Jeff's vice president of sales and marketing decided to take another opportunity and was replaced by a new vice president of sales and marketing. Shortly thereafter, we were fired. The reason: lack of a return on investment.

I was floored!

Upon hearing the news, I called Jeff and asked for more details. Jeff mentioned that we had done good work, but at the end of the day, he did not feel marketing was driving the value that he had hoped for. When I mentioned the $30 million contract and marketing's role in the process, he stated, "Our sales team would have landed that project anyway."

At that moment, I realized we had a big issue. We couldn't prove our value. Expectations were off and not clearly defined.

If we could not retain a client that we helped to secure $30 million, especially when that client was a family member, we needed to change. And change we did.

We had to change, just as you have to.

PART ONE

CHALLENGING YOUR MARKETING PARADIGM

ONE

PLAY STUPID GAMES, WIN STUPID PRIZES

Early in my marketing career, I made a lot of mistakes. Those mistakes cost my company a lot of money, but worse than losing money, I lost valuable time. Time is something you cannot get back. Time is something we don't have the luxury of squandering.

To scale a manufacturing business or your marketing operation, time and timing are critical. You cannot wait months or years hoping for success. This is true for all the clients I have served over the past twenty-plus years. They are sick and tired of wasting time and money on marketing that does not propel their companies forward. How often have you wished you could rewind the clock and get a do-over or hit "command-Z" on your computer to erase the last six months of wasted effort?

To illustrate how critical it is to avoid playing stupid games, get out a pen and paper, and write down in the table three failed marketing initiatives that you have launched. Record the financial investment and the time wasted for each. Add them up. It's a big number. Most likely, it's in the tens of thousands or hundreds of thousands of dollars wasted and years of lost opportunities. The unfortunate truth is that we have all been there. If you truly cannot think of anything to fill the blanks in the table, then you should be writing your own book and throwing this one away.

Marketing Initiative	Time Taken to Build, Launch, and Assess Outcomes	Estimated Cost of the Entire Process, Including Salaries and External Costs
Example: Developed a new website	Six months	Internal time cost: $15,000 Outsourced vendors: $125,000 Total: $140,000
	Total time:	Total cost:

When considering these failed initiatives, it's important to locate the source of each failure. To do so, consider the following:

- Did you hire the wrong marketing manager, only to find out later that they didn't really know their stuff?
- Did you launch a new website to drive leads and awareness, only to realize nothing improved?
- Did you hire an agency that did not perform?
- Did you invest in a software that you never or barely used?

What was the opportunity cost due to these mistakes? What progress or successes would your company have experienced if the marketing effort had worked as desired? Hint: it's another large amount of money squandered.

Often it takes more than a year to assess the success or failure of a marketing initiative. Personally, I've wasted years and hundreds of thousands of dollars. It sucks.

When marketing makes guesses and plays stupid games, even when those games are played with the best of intentions, you win stupid prizes. But it does not have to be this way. What if you could avoid these mistakes?

The bulk of your marketing problems are rooted in a lack of the proper **people**, **strategies**, **systems**, and **software** to move the needle.

WHY YOU ARE NOT GETTING A MEASURABLE RETURN ON YOUR MARKETING INVESTMENT

Let's face it: marketing is hard. Marketing is a complex science consisting of multichannel strategies, technologies, tactics, artistic flair, timing, and messaging. It requires a sophisticated team of experts to drive the results leadership expects.

Having worked with hundreds of small to midsize companies, I have found they face two primary marketing issues:

1. They often don't have the budget to implement the proper marketing infrastructure needed for success: people, strategies, systems, and software.

Unfortunately, corporate budgets rarely support marketing with the proper funding due to lagging past performance and a belief that marketing is a necessary evil. I've actually had more than one business owner tell me that they believe marketing is smoke and mirrors. This pissed me off, but I didn't blame them. It was all that they had experienced.

Lower budgets mean marketing teams with insufficient resources to get the job done. This is akin to running a marathon without running shoes or training. It can be done, but it will really suck along the way.

2. Marketing leaders often don't know how to build the proper infrastructure needed for success: **people**, **strategies**, **systems**, and **software**.

The result is underperformance, wasted time, wasted money, and frustration. Typically, this results in pressure from leadership. Marketers then start working harder and put in more time focusing on more tactics and more output. They fall into the belief that more blogs, more videos, more social posts, more emails—more, more, more—will drive greater results.

You can see where this is going.

Marketing leaders and executives become addicted to the rhythm and cadence of inefficient productivity and loss-leader statistics. In turn, they expect "more, more, more." The result is a tactical marketing effort driven by output versus outcomes. I call this whack-a-mole-style marketing. Whack-a-mole marketing is where you respond to whatever pops up, just like the whack-a-mole arcade game. It's reactive marketing and often lacks a marketing strategy.

The "more, more, more" approach may drive a short-term spike in metrics, but it rarely drives long-term return on investment.

If your marketing team is not following a formal marketing strategy that is defined in writing and aligns specific tactics to specific objectives, then you are well on your way to insanity.

"More, more, more" also burns out the marketing team, leading to turnover, culture issues, lost institutional knowledge, and increased costs—the exact opposite of the objective!

The good news is that it's not your fault or your leadership team's fault. It's just what happens when marketing is not aligned with a comprehensive plan supported by **people**, **strategies**, **systems**, and **software**.

If the above hits home, you are not alone. We see this every day. The good news is that there is a solution. It's not easy, but if you follow the science outlined in this book, your marketing issues will be a thing of the past. You can be the hero who drives the company forward!

For the methodologies in this book to work, you have to be open and trust the process. Sometimes this may mean taking two steps back to take one step forward.

MORE, MORE, MORE

We were retained by a large, privately held company to assist in improving sales leads and new customers, with the expectation they would attain a measurable return on investment. We were stoked. I really liked working with this company and all the people we met and worked with, including the senior executives. However, after working with them for over a year, we learned that some companies just cannot be helped.

The company had several divisions, and they all competed with one another for sales. It was very odd. Marketing was not driving the desired results, and they were spending millions of dollars on recruiting, training, and replacing salespeople each year. While this company was very successful, it was a mess—one of the most unorganized and fractured organizations we have ever worked with.

THE GREAT 8 PILLARS

The first thing we did was assess the existing marketing team's operational infrastructure via our Diagnostic and Roadmap process (more on that later in the book). We found that the marketing team, with just under ten full-time employees, was not operating from a formal marketing strategy. They were focusing on output versus outcomes. More blogs, more videos, more social media, and so on.

Over the course of our relationship, all the members of their marketing team communicated that they were burned out and frustrated. There was a lot of finger-pointing and blaming. Their manager, the marketing leader, was driving them into the ground. He was an old-school marketer and couldn't let go of the whack-a-mole-style approach he had been using for the last thirty years.

The end result? We were never able to get the marketing leader onboard. We did build out a formal marketing strategy and implemented the systems required for success. Unfortunately, we were met with resistance at every step of the process. Ultimately, they bailed out and kept doing things the way they always had. More, more, more.

T W O

WHAT IS AN ROI-DRIVEN MARKETING OPERATION?

M any years ago, I was at a conference where the keynote speaker said, "Sales is the lifeblood of a company, and marketing is arts and crafts." As a marketer, I was infuriated. How could he say that? How could such an accomplished leader and speaker not recognize the value of marketing? Begrudgingly, I also knew in my heart that he was somewhat right. Salespeople got all the credit. They were the ones who secured new contracts and customers for their businesses. Salespeople owned the relationships. Marketers operated behind the scenes and were seen as a necessary evil.

Over the last fifteen years, this has grown to no longer be the case. Today, you can effectively measure a return on your marketing investment. Marketers can prove their impact on corporate growth. Unfortunately, many marketers were not taught ROI-driven marketing in college due to the aging professors who didn't have real-world experience in today's business climate. The result is that many marketers are still operating in decades-old methodologies of brand awareness marketing and reporting on vanity metrics such as impressions, visits, or touches.

The ROI-Driven Marketing Operation is your goal; it's where you need to be. Why? ROI-driven marketing solves all your marketing problems. When you consistently deliver ROI, you sleep better at night, and your team spends less time on tactical work that doesn't produce results. Your team's culture improves, and turnover is reduced. You attain clarity and improve efficiencies with the proper tools, systems, and standard operating procedures.

If ROI-driven marketing is new to you, fear not. The Great 8 Pillars and over one hundred coordinating gold standards outlined in this book are designed to get you to a point where:

1. **You attain a measurable return on investment from marketing**. We've all likely heard this phrase from the movie *Field of Dreams*: "If you build it, they will come." Most marketers believe this, but in reality, it does not happen. For real marketing ROI, you must build it, nurture it, tweak it, analyze it, and repeat. Real marketing ROI comes from an integrated marketing strategy supported by the right **people, strategies, systems**, and **software**.

2. **You are no longer implementing whack-a-mole-style tactical marketing**. Many companies' marketing approach consists of tactical busywork. They believe that more is better. This is a sure way to waste a lot of time and money. The ROI-Driven Marketing Operation follows a strategic marketing plan and measures every marketing tactic to determine what works and what doesn't. You continually optimize your marketing and are able to make smarter decisions and eliminate wasted time and money.

3. **You operate in a culture of clarity and transparency where everyone knows what role**

they're playing. When accountability isn't clearly defined, we find that people can hide behind facade numbers or feel the freedom to point fingers at others. A marketing-driven operation eliminates excuses and finger-pointing. Everyone knows what they're accountable for and what role they play in the game.

4. **Marketing and sales teams are aligned**. If sales is the lifeblood of your company, marketing is the blood pressure. They go hand in hand. Today, marketing should be considered pre-sales or sales enablement. If your marketing and sales teams are operating in silos, it's hard to attain real ROI. Regardless of your industry or company size, marketing and sales must act as one revenue team. Your goal is to cultivate an environment where sales and marketing are leveraging the same tools and data, working hand in hand, and attaining success together for the growth of the company.

5. **You can make marketing decisions faster and more accurately**. With the right **people**, **strategies**, **systems**, and **software** in place, sales

and marketing leadership gains visibility of what's working and what's not, which allows for the following:

    a. Sound judgment on key marketing initiatives

    b. Doubling down on what's working and abandoning what's not—and doing so faster

    c. Identifying where the gaps are between sales and marketing and what needs to be improved

When you begin to implement these eight pillars, you'll be better able to accurately forecast the following:

- Your marketing ROI
- How each marketing channel is performing (social, organic, direct, inbound, etc.)
- What your top-performing marketing tactics are
- Who on the team is working
- What is working
- Why it's working
- Marketing versus sales challenges
- Lead sources and lead counts
- Lead conversion rates per channel

The ROI-Driven Marketing Operation is where you deliver real results for the company you serve. It's where you stop focusing exclusively on tactical efforts and start to move the needle. It's where you start to sleep at night again. It's where your team members stop getting burned out and resigning. It's where your company is able to scale and you become a marketing superhero!

Do you have what it takes to develop an ROI-Driven Marketing Operation? Ask yourself these questions:

1. Is your business looking to scale and grow?
2. Does your company have the proper funds to invest in its marketing operations?
3. Is leadership willing to challenge the status quo?
4. Is leadership willing to admit that its value proposition may need work?
5. Are you willing to trust the process and stop doing tactical vanity marketing?
6. Are you sick and tired of wasting time and money on marketing that does not work?
7. Are you experiencing turnover in your marketing staff or agencies?
8. Is marketing seen as an investment, not an expense?

9. Are your salespeople not hitting their sales goals?
10. Are you finding it harder to connect with buyers and earn their attention?

If you answered yes to at least eight of these questions, congratulations! You are ready for ROI-driven marketing. If you answered no to three or more of these questions, you may want to rethink things. ROI-driven marketing is an investment in time and money. If your company is not ready to embrace this effort, you may find yourself pushing a boulder uphill.

As we'll see in Chapter 3, managing executive expectations is the responsibility of every good marketing leader, and doing so effectively can mean better results for you and your team.

THREE

EXECUTIVE PERSPECTIVES

There is no such thing as a business expense.
All "expenses" in business are investments
that must provide a measurable return.
−UNKNOWN

Trust me when I say that executive leadership expects to make significantly more money than what they invest in marketing. They want a marketing return on investment (ROI). It's the number-one reason that they reach out to my firm. The conversation usually goes like this:

Executive: Thank you for taking my call. I'm reaching out because we need help. We are not seeing the results we expected from marketing. We've invested a significant amount of money, time, and resources. We are disappointed with the results and the lack of progress. Can you help us?

Me: When you say you are not seeing results, what are you seeing? Can you provide more detail?

Executive: We are doing a lot more marketing and creating a ton of content. We built a new website too. The marketing reports show some improvement in metrics, but we are not landing any measurable new sales. We expected to land more business from marketing, and it's just not happening. I am very frustrated. Our agency (or internal marketing team) told us to trust them, and now I have lost all confidence.

I've heard this over and over from business owners, CEOs, and presidents. Expectation levels are high.

The problem is that marketing ROI has traditionally been very hard to measure, and many marketers don't agree on the difference between measurable goals that move the business forward and vanity metrics and key performance indicators (KPIs). Vanity metrics and KPIs are often the same thing. They inform the effectiveness of a tactical implementation. However, marketers often report to executives on KPIs as marketing's measurement of success, not the actual return on investment from marketing. When this happens, I call it vanity metrics because these metrics don't mean anything to the growth of the company if they are not directly tied to increased sales or customer loyalty. If your marketing reports are filled with these vanity metrics, it's time to reassess your reporting criteria.

Manufacturing executives don't care about conversion rates, email open rates, and website traffic increases. These are things marketers care about because they help identify the direction of your marketing efforts, but they are not metrics that speak to ROI. Executives care only about revenue generated from the marketing effort, and it's up to you, as a marketer, to prove it.

As a business owner, I have had the privilege of meeting many other manufacturing owners, CEOs, presidents, and executives. Although most of these leaders are passionate, caring people, they carry a significant amount of personal risk. Often they operate in personal debt or give up their personal lives to make their companies successful. When things go bad and times are tough, they are usually the ones who take the hit first. Almost every business owner I know has been deeply in debt, gone bankrupt at one point, or not taken a paycheck to keep their company afloat.

A couple of years ago, one of my clients pulled me aside and told me that our marketing work had saved his company. Prior to hiring us, he had cashed in his 401(k) retirement savings to make payroll, and the bank was calling on his loan. It was a dire time for him. You can imagine just how important his investment in marketing was.

Even if your business is not in such dire financial circumstances, you can guarantee that the leadership team is expecting you to deliver.

WHY EXECUTIVES BECOME INVOLVED IN MARKETING

Executive leaders (C-suite) have better things to do with their time than get involved in the details of marketing. They have a lot of pressure on their shoulders to keep the company growing and profitable. A large majority do not want to be involved in marketing, nor do they want to micromanage the marketing team. When an executive becomes mired in the marketing program, there are typically four primary reasons:

1. **They want harmony**. Executive leadership is looking to implement a larger strategy that involves marketing, and they want to ensure all systems are working in harmony. They may simply want to understand the whys behind the marketing strategy and may be questioning the tactics being implemented. Messaging, target audiences, and brand are all part of a system that they are looking to control. If an executive is seeking harmony, this is a good thing. They are just making sure that everyone is on the same page regarding the company's direction.

2. **They want to understand**. Executives don't always see the whys behind the marketing strategy or the tactics being implemented. What they do see are micro-components of their company's marketing from a tactical perspective. In a vacuum, the tactics may not make sense, and it can cause heartburn for the executive if the tactic is not on par with the strategic direction of the company. Often the executive just needs a better understanding of what you are doing and why to gain confidence in your program.

THE GREAT 8 PILLARS

3. **There is a change of executive control.** When a
    new executive leader is hired or promoted, they
    are looking to make sure that their vision is going
    to be implemented. After all, they were hired
    for a reason, and they have an accountability
    to perform. If this person has control over sales
    and marketing, you can bet that they will be
    asking a lot of questions, often challenging past
    marketing decisions and performance reports. In
    this situation, you must be on your toes. Don't get
    defensive. Be open to shifting gears, and get on
    the same page.

4. **They are not getting value.** Marketing can be a
    big line item on the corporate financial books, and
    when results are not being achieved, executives
    will take control. When marketing efforts are not
    providing a return on investment, it looks bad for
    the executive (and the marketing team). If your
    executive has taken control and is starting to
    micromanage the marketing due to a lack of value,
    you should be concerned. They are taking control
    because they have lost confidence in your ability to
    drive the desired results.

If you have experienced or are experiencing any of the four issues above, the first thing you must do is take control of the situation. If you don't take control and prove that you have a strategic plan, the executive will. Typically, this is illustrated by the executive calling the shots and micromanaging the marketing direction. When this happens, your future employment is uncertain. This usually results in highly tactical initiatives, such as:

- "We need better SEO. I want to rank number one in Google for XYZ search term."
- "We need to do more video marketing."
- "I want to go viral."
- "We need more social media outreach."
- "We need to implement a PR campaign."

The list goes on and on.

Don't fall into these traps! Yes, your executive leader may be asking for specifics, but I have seen it over and over: you attain their specific goal, and they are still not happy. Why? Because what they really wanted was cold, hard cash. They really wanted sales revenue and thought that they knew what marketing tactic would deliver it. When it fails to deliver the goods, they make changes, fire team members, change agencies, or ask for a new focus on another tactic.

Whack-a-mole marketing!

As marketers, you must ensure your efforts are moving the company's growth forward. Otherwise, you are an expense that will eventually be cut.

What you must do is sit down with the executive or the entire leadership team and reset. The following are some examples of how to navigate the situation:

1. **Ask them what they want, and then ask why**. "Why do you want to rank number one in Google? Why do you want a new website? Why do you want more SEO?" If you ask why enough times, you will find that what they really want is increased sales revenue. They want to grow and outperform the competition. Period. End of story. Once you determine that, you can begin to build a plan that works to accomplish the goal.

2. **Pull together the past twelve to twenty-four months of marketing initiatives, and walk them through the plan**. Make sure you have supporting data to illustrate *why* you made the decisions

you did. If possible, aggregate data and reports to illustrate the progress marketing has made. Admit which initiatives failed and how you adjusted. If you can't make this step happen, it's likely because there was no marketing strategy to begin with or you didn't have the tracking mechanisms in place to attain data.

3. **If there has been a change in executive control and a new executive is in charge of the marketing direction, be open to the option of completely revamping the marketing strategy**. New executives bring new ideas, new contacts, and new relationships. You may find that your marketing program may take a whole new direction.

Once it is clearly laid out that more sales revenue is the objective and performance is expected, it's time to develop a strategy to get there.

So let's get started on giving them what they want.

PART TWO

BUILDING AN ROI-DRIVEN MARKETING OPERATION

FOUR

THE DIAGNOSTIC AND ROADMAP

More than likely, your current marketing efforts have some true merit. You are probably doing many things very well, and you just need to connect the dots and fill in the blanks to achieve real marketing ROI.

Any successful journey starts with knowing where you are today and where you want to go tomorrow. The first step is to diagnose where your marketing operation stands today against:

- Industry gold standards

- Best practices
- Standard operating procedures

Once you have done this, you can build a roadmap to guide your efforts for the future.

The ROI-Driven Marketing Diagnostic and Roadmap exists to bring three things to light:

1. **Your Organization's Current Marketing State**: You can't get where you want to go if you don't know where you are coming from. The Diagnostic and Roadmap will provide a clear picture of your organization's current marketing state so you know what needs work.

2. **Where You Want to Be**: Business leaders are looking for a utopia where business grows in routine processes and rhythms. Unfortunately, most don't have even a faint idea of what that utopia looks like, especially when it comes to marketing. The Diagnostic and Roadmap will show you.

3. **How You're Going to Get There**: Based on your marketing's current state, the Diagnostic and

Roadmap will tell you everything you need to do (and in what order) to build an ROI-Driven Marketing Operation. This is a "Diagnose + Prescribe" document. It tells you where you're at (diagnosis) and where you want to be and provides a plan on how you'll get there (prescription).

GET VULNERABLE

All progress starts with getting vulnerable and honestly assessing your current marketing operational state. It's okay to admit fault or a lack of knowledge or that past efforts have not worked as well as you had hoped. If you do not accurately assess your current situation, then your starting point will be off, and attaining a 10X ROI will be very difficult, if not impossible. The goal is to make your marketing team successful by building a truly remarkable marketing operation. Pride and saving face can only get in the way.

The Ultimate 10X ROI Marketing Diagnostic and Roadmap Assessment

We have good news for you. We have a free online template you can use to diagnose your current marketing operational state against the gold standards, industry best practices, and standard operating procedures. This template will guide you through each step of the diagnosis process. Upon completion, you will have a solid understanding of where you are and where you need to improve.

To get started, access the Ultimate 10X ROI Marketing Diagnostic and Roadmap Assessment from our website, and begin to diagnose your current marketing state. You can find this template at *www.G8P.co* in our resource section. Once you have downloaded the assessment, follow the instructions provided.

What you will need:

- Access to your Google Analytics account
- Access to your website content management system
- Access to your customer relationship management (CRM) software
- An honest and open mind

Once you have completed the assessment, a roadmap will be generated based on your inputs. This roadmap will provide the general direction and an order of priorities in building your ROI-Driven Marketing Operation.

You may find the roadmap to be a valuable tool in presenting your future goals, challenges, and obstacles to senior management. Alternatively, you can use the road-map as your personal guide to success! The roadmap is just a guide to help you along the way. Regardless of your roadmap results, we recommend that you read each chapter of this book carefully and use the information provided herein to begin working on your ROI-Driven Marketing Operation.

If any of your eight pillars is not well rooted in the gold standards, then your chances of attaining a 10X ROI are significantly hindered. Over the following days, weeks, and months, take extra time to invest in each pillar. Make adjustments as you go, and remember this is a marathon, not a sprint.

Challenge yourself to really home in and ask the right questions.

Trust me when I say that building this infrastructure will provide the freedom, knowledge, and success you have been looking for. A marketing strategy rooted in the Great 8 Pillars will revolutionize your  perspective of marketing while saving you time, money, and the dread of directionless marketing discussions with leadership. The next chapter will introduce you to those eight pillars and how they can reshape your professional life.

THE GREAT 8 PILLARS OF ROI-DRIVEN MARKETING

I t all started in 2010 when we lost a big client. Over the following years, we worked tirelessly to drive real, measurable results for our clients. Did we sometimes fail? Yes, we did, but we also moved the needle and delivered great results for many of our clients. We honed our processes, measured everything, and continuously improved.

Let's fast forward to 2019. I had just hired John, our new vice president of client services. John is a great guy and is always looking for "true north." He has an incredible ability to see through the clutter, find truth, and define reality. True to John's disposition, he pulled me aside several weeks after he started with SyncShow (my agency) and began asking deep questions.

> John: Hey, Chris, I wanted to talk to you about the results we claim to be delivering for our clients. I've worked at several agencies, both large and small, and no one is delivering results like you are claiming at SyncShow. Do we really deliver the numbers that we are claiming?
>
> Me: It's a great question, and I am glad you asked. The numbers we reference in our marketing and sales presentations are specific client or aggregate data pulled from actual client work. They are accurate, but, admittedly, we have not pulled new data in over a year. What do you think about diving into more recent data and finding out what our numbers are now and reporting back to me? It would be great to see how we are trending.
>
> John: I'm on it. Give me a couple of weeks to dig in.

A couple of weeks later, John scheduled a meeting with me, and as he walked into the room, he had a big smile on his face.

> John: So remember you asked me to dive into our client data and aggregate the performance measurements?

Well, I did, and you were right. We are really good.
But I didn't realize just how good.

Me: That's great news. What did you find?

John: I looked back at the past two years of data. I measured all of our clients' results relative to the goals agreed to at the beginning of each client's engagement. What I found was astonishing. We met or exceeded client goals 95 percent of the time—often blowing away the target goals and in many cases delivering an ROI in excess of 10X!

Me: That's awesome. So the next big question is exactly how are we doing it? We must be doing something right, something that other agencies are not doing. What do you think about really diving deep and mapping out exactly what we are doing and what we are not doing?

John: I think we are on to something. It's going to be a big project, but well worth it. Let's do it!

It was at this time that we realized we were really good cooks but never wrote down our recipes. And so began an eighteen-month deep-dive analysis into everything marketing as we knew it. We looked at every *how* and *why*. We looked at *what* tools, processes, and tactics we were implementing and *when*, based on the client's starting point compared to their goals. We looked at our proprietary processes and the decades of knowledge collected along the way.

BUILDING A STRONG FOUNDATION

When the dust settled, we distilled everything we were doing into eight primary marketing categories we call pillars. We found that if best practices were not followed in any of these categories, marketing results often lagged.

We also found that some categories are so important to attaining ROI that if they are not done well, then success is practically impossible.

So we set off to research and document the gold standards in each category. These gold standards are generally accepted marketing industry metrics, best practices as recommended by Google and other industry leaders, and, of course, our learnings over two decades.

The result is the Great 8 Pillars of ROI-Driven Marketing and over one hundred gold standards. Our clients now follow this methodology, and it works time and time again.

With that, I am excited to introduce to you the Great 8 Pillars of ROI-Driven Marketing. These pillars are listed in order of importance. They have been specifically constructed in this order to assist you in a step-by-step chronological path to developing your marketing roadmap to the ROI-Driven Marketing Operation.

- **Pillar 1: Goals, KPIs, and Industry Benchmarks— Defining Your 10X.** We start with goal setting, key performance indicators, and industry benchmarks to define true north.

- **Pillar 2: Value Proposition, Messaging, and Branding**. If your value proposition sucks, your marketing won't produce the results you desire.

- **Pillar 3: Marketing Strategy**. We guide you through building a marketing strategy your executive team will love.

- **Pillar 4: Marketing Team Structure**. Without the right team, your marketing strategy cannot be implemented. We help you build your marketing dream team.

- **Pillar 5: Website**. Beyond the online brochure, we show you how to attain a lead generation machine.

- **Pillar 6: Analytics and Reporting**. Measure twice, cut once. Learn how to attain the proper analytics and what you should be reporting on.

- **Pillar 7: Technology Stack**. We outline the tools and software required for success.

- **Pillar 8: Templates and Guides**. We provide the key assets to increase productivity.

The eight pillars were derived from over thirty different areas of marketing. Your specific strategy may call for you to pull in other areas of marketing, such as paid advertising, account-based marketing, and the like. The reason we focused on these eight categories is that we believe they are the foundation of ROI-driven marketing. They are also the key areas that most organizations are lacking in.

GOING FOR THE GOLD

Now that you have a basic understanding of what the Great 8 Pillars are, it's time to introduce you to the gold standards. For each of the pillars, we defined a checklist of gold standards to ensure each pillar is properly implemented.

These gold standards will be your guide in implementation. As you progress through the following chapters, spend some time considering each set of gold standards and how you might begin to incorporate them into your work practices.

The following journey illustration will help you envision your future path. Remember to trust the process. It works!

By now you are probably chomping at the bit to jump in and get started, but remember, this is a marathon, not a sprint. As I mentioned in the introduction, the methodologies included herein are not quick-fix tactics. It may take you six to twelve months or more to achieve the operational infrastructure you desire. Just remember that the process works. If you follow the process outlined in this book, I guarantee you will see success. Just stick with it.

If you need help along the way, visit our website for additional information, blog articles, videos, tools, and templates. And if you need extra help, reach out to one of our certified Great 8 marketing guides to help you.

GOALS, KPIS, AND INDUSTRY BENCHMARKS
DEFINING YOUR 10X

Now that you've completed your Ultimate 10X ROI Marketing Diagnostic and Roadmap Assessment, you're ready to define your big hairy audacious 10X ROI marketing goal. We will also assist you in developing a list of key performance indicators (KPIs) related to your goal for tracking and reporting purposes.

Industry benchmarks are also a critical piece of this puzzle. When creating your KPIs to support goal attainment, look to some standard industry benchmarks we use to help guide KPI objectives. These benchmarks are best used as targets to measure your effectiveness. Remember that industry benchmarks may not be available for your specific manufacturing niche. That's okay. If benchmark data is not available, choose a niche that is similar to yours. Benchmark data changes year over year. We recommend you do a little research for benchmarks for your specific industry to accomplish this step.

DEFINING YOUR 10X

The first step in delivering a 10X return on marketing investment is to calculate your ROI goal. This should be a simple task and is easily accomplished by asking for the marketing budget. Most companies have a formal budget for each department. If not, you can use the outline below to complete a basic formula and build a budget for ROI analysis purposes.

The objective is to determine how much money is going to be spent on marketing over the calendar year or how much has been spent in the previous calendar year for comparison purposes.

The budget should include *all* expenses attributed to marketing. If you have a department budget provided to you, make sure it includes the line items below.

The average B2B manufacturing company spends approximately 6 to 7 percent of their revenues on marketing. The numbers in the table represent a company with approximately $10 million in revenues and are for illustrative purposes only. They are not meant to provide direction on where your budget should be spent.

Item	Cost
Marketing team salaries, including benefits, taxes, equipment (if you don't have this detailed information, make some assumptions on salaries and add 20 percent)	1 full-time marketer salary = $95,000 1 full-time marketer salary = $65,000 Total = $160,000 × 1.20% = $192,000 total human resources
Advertising and sponsorship expenses	$100,000
Marketing technology, software, tool costs, subscriptions	$36,500
Vendor costs	$160,000
Trade shows, events, webinar costs	$50,000
Team member training (conferences, certifications)	$6,000
Miscellaneous marketing expenses	$25,500
Website and hosting costs	$30,000
Subtotal	**$600,000**
Multiply by 10	× 10
10X ROI Goal	**$6,000,000**

The table illustrates a typical company's marketing budget. The first step in defining your 10X ROI goal is to download our 10X ROI Goal Template and fill in the blanks. You can find this template at *www.G8P.co* in our resource section.

Assuming you have completed your 10X ROI template, you now have a target that is a 10X return on investment. You may be asking yourself, "Why 10X? Why not 3X or 5X ROI?" To keep it simple, we use 10X ROI. Anyone will tell you that a 10X ROI is incredibly lofty, and it is. However, it is doable. Regardless, lofty goals deliver lofty results. Even if you fall short of the goal, you are way ahead of where you are today and can work to build upon your successes.

Still, we do recommend keeping this goal to yourself or within the marketing team. It is your personal objective. You don't want to set expectations too high for your executive leaders. Experience has shown that if you share a 10X goal with your executive team and fall short, they won't appreciate 2X or 3X results, which are also incredible.

IDENTIFYING YOUR ROI CURRENT STATE

Now that you have a 10X ROI goal, it's time to identify your marketing ROI current state. Use the table as a guide for your calculations.

Marketing Key Performance Indicator	Current Data	Current Conversion Rates
Current website traffic per month *(Make sure to filter out your company's IP address or any other traffic that is not related to new customers.)*	2,500	
Website Leads Generated per month *(To make this simple, we consider a "lead" anyone who converts on the website. Sometimes this means a solicitation or current customer.)*	12	= 0.0048% conversion rate
Website Marketing-Qualified Leads (MQL) generated per month *(An MQL is a lead who meets your ideal customer profile and buyer persona profile.)*	6	Lead to MQL conversion rate = 50%
Website Sales-Qualified Leads (SQL) generated per month *(An SQL is a lead who meets your ideal customer profile and buyer persona profile and is someone sales wants to talk to.)*	2	MQL to SQL conversion rate = 33%

It's important to note that most companies I have worked with don't have all of this data readily available. If this is the case for you, enter "best guess" data. You may need to ask the sales leader for this information; however, it is good to ask other executives as well. Often, executives disagree over these numbers, and you need one center of truth. Ideally, these numbers should be tracked by both sales and marketing teams. Doing so will enable you to attain more accurate data in the future.

Using the same spreadsheet as previously, click on the Current Data KPI tab and fill in the blanks.

Sales Pipeline

Our experience shows that some companies have a sales pipeline formally defined and others don't. If your organization does, there may be several steps in the pipeline, or it may be very simple. The objective in this step is to understand and document (to the best of your ability) what sales data illustrates.

This table illustrates a marketing operation that is delivering $150,000 in annual revenue on a $600,000 budget, equating to a $450,000 loss per year! This means that the marketing operation is an expense on the corporate books and not an investment. Think of your marketing department as if it were a separate company. Under this scenario, the company is losing a lot of money, and a profitless company means you will be out of business soon. If, upon completion of this exercise, you find that your marketing department is in a similar situation, you should be concerned.

Sales Pipeline	Current Data	Current Conversion Rates
Sales-Qualified Leads that go to Proposal	50%	2 SQLs per month = 1 Proposal per month
Proposal to Closed Won	50%	1 win every other month
Average Order Value (Your sales leader will need to provide this.)	$25,000	Current estimated annual revenue from marketing = $150,000
Customer Lifetime Value (How much revenue does your average client bring to your organization for the lifetime of their account?)	$250,000	Current lifetime estimated value from marketing = $1,500,000

As you fill in the blanks for your organization, you will gain a much stronger understanding of how you should be thinking and planning. Your sales operation may be more complex or simpler. By using this basic table, you will get a strong idea of your current marketing ROI (or lack thereof).

Once you have completed the template, save it for future reference.

DEFINING YOUR KEY PERFORMANCE INDICATORS

The next step is to break down the ROI-driven key performance indicators that will help you to focus your future marketing strategy. To do this, we have to do some backward math. We basically have turned the above chart upside down and reordered it, last to first. It's really quite simple—just follow along the outline below and fill in your numbers.

Using the same spreadsheet as before, click on the KPI tab and fill in the blanks. For illustrative purposes, we cut the table in half to focus on the sales pipeline KPIs first. This will help you to define the sales-qualified leads marketing must deliver.

10X ROI Goal: $6,000,000

Sales Pipeline		
Customer Lifetime Value *(How much revenue does your average client bring to your organization for the lifetime of their account?)*	$250,000 *(same as above)*	$6,000,000/$250,000 = 24 new customers
Average Order Value *(Your sales leader will need to provide this.)*	$25,000 *(same as above)*	Future estimated annual revenue from marketing: 24 × $25,000 = $600,000
Proposal to Closed Won	50% *(same as above)*	24/12 months = 2 new customers per month
Sales-Qualified Leads that go to Proposal	50% *(same as above)*	8 SQLs per month = 4 Proposals/month

Congratulations! You now have specific SQL goals to deliver a 10X ROI.

> *Note: When looking at marketing spend versus annual reve-*
> *nues, the formula above illustrates a breakeven on ROI in the*
> *first year ($600,000). Many marketers and executives don't*
> *consider the customer lifetime value. The customer lifetime*
> *value is the key to a 10X ROI. Let me explain this a bit further.*
> *Marketing ROI is measured primarily by a simple equation:*
>
> *Marketing Revenue Earned – Marketing $$$ Spent = ROI*
>
> *Marketing revenue earned typically means new clients.*
> *These clients often drive revenue to your company over a*
> *period of years, not just one time. You must factor in the long-*
> *term value of these new clients, which is measured by cus-*
> *tomer lifetime value.*

Now that you have the SQL numbers, you can complete the backward math to formulate your specific marketing key performance indicators.

As stated above, your ROI must consider customer lifetime value; however, we also recognize that executives don't always see it this way. We recommend that you increase the numbers to plan for a 3X ROI, not including customer lifetime value, within the first year. This will help you work toward an ROI goal that executives will buy into. In the illustration above, this would equate to $1,800,000 in first-year annual revenues rather than $600,000.

Now we must continue the reverse math process and define how many leads, MQLs, SQLs, and website visitors you will need for success.

Using the same spreadsheet as before, click on the Marketing KPI tab and fill in the blanks.

Key Performance Indicator	Example Data	Current Conversion Rates
Website Sales-Qualified Leads (SQLs) generated per month *(An SQL is a lead who meets your ideal customer profile and buyer persona profile and is someone sales wants to talk to.)*	8 *(same as above)*	MQL to SQL conversion rate = 33% *(same as above)*
Website Marketing-Qualified Leads (MQLs) generated per month *(An MQL is a lead who meets your ideal customer profile and buyer persona profile.)*	24 *(8 SQLs is 33% of 24)*	Lead to MQL conversion rate = 50% *(same as above)*

Website Leads Generated per month (To make this simple, we consider a "lead" anyone who converts on the website. Sometimes this means a solicitation or current customer.)	48 (24 MQLs is 50% of 48)	Conversion rate = 0.0048% (same as above)
Current Website Traffic per month (Make sure to filter out your company's IP address or any other traffic that is not related to new customers.)	10,000	N/A

Congratulations! By completing this process, you now have documented ROI SMART (specific, measurable, attainable, realistic, and timely) goals and supporting ROI-driven key performance indicators. These goals and KPIs should be tracked and reported on regularly.

You may be thinking that 10,000 website visitors per month is not attainable, and you are probably correct (at least in the short term). To realistically accomplish the goal in this illustration, we have to adjust the website visitor-to-lead conversion rate.

The conversion rate in the illustration above is forty-eight hundredths of 1 percent (0.0048). I specifically included a conversion rate this low because it is not uncommon for us to see such a low conversion rate for companies that have not focused on conversion rate optimization.

The B2B industry benchmark for website visitors-to-lead conversion rate is 2.5 to 5 percent.

Let's redo the math using the bottom end of the industry benchmark.

Using the same spreadsheet as before, click on the Conversion Rates tab and fill in the blanks.

Key Performance Indicator	Example Data	Current Conversion Rates
Website Sales-Qualified Leads (SQLs) generated per month (*An SQL is a lead who meets your ideal customer profile and buyer persona profile and is someone sales wants to talk to.*)	8 *(same as above)*	MQL to SQL conversion rate = 33% *(same as above)*
Website Marketing-Qualified Leads (MQLs) generated per month (*An MQL is a lead who meets your ideal customer profile and buyer persona profile.*)	24 *(8 SQLs is 33% of 24)* *(same as above)*	Lead to MQL conversion rate = 50% *(same as above)*
Website Leads Generated per month (*To make this simple, we consider a "lead" anyone who converts on the website. Sometimes this means a solicitation or current customer.*)	48 *(24 MQLs is 50% of 48)* *(same as above)*	Conversion rate = 2.5%
Current Website Traffic per month (*Make sure to filter out your company's IP address or any other traffic that is not related to new customers.*)	1,920	N/A

Wow! By focusing on your conversion rate and bringing it up to the bottom end of industry benchmarks, you can actually reduce your traffic from your current state while driving the success you wish for. Now we're talking!

For most marketers, the ability to reach your ROI goal lies in both traffic increases and conversion rate optimization. This is a great example of outcomes over output. Many marketers would have just focused on getting more traffic. More. More. More. More does not work!

LESSON LEARNED
GARBAGE IN, GARBAGE OUT

Years ago, we were working with a fast-growing client. They were kicking ass, and their marketing team was driving awareness at an incredible rate (or so we thought). Website visits were increasing by 5X year over year. Their executive team was receiving monthly marketing reports, and everyone was very happy.

Then we found it.

Early in our engagement, our team discovered that their website traffic was counting user log-ins. At this point, the company had hundreds of customers logging in to their site. These clients often logged in each day, sometimes multiple times per day. This was what was causing such dramatic increases in website traffic. No one had ever filtered out this traffic from their analytics report.

We informed the marketing director of our findings, and she was completely deflated. The real website traffic had actually been stagnant over the previous years. She had been pumping up traffic growth to her leadership team for years, and now it was all meaningless. I felt really sorry for her.

The good news is that we were able to filter this traffic from their reports and build a solid plan for moving forward. Their visitor-to-lead conversion rate also increased. Unfortunately, she didn't have the heart (or guts) to admit the error to her leadership team. Future executive reports omitted the filtered data. Personally, I didn't blame her; I don't know if I would have had the guts either.

It has been more than five years, and she is still working at that company doing an amazing job. She is now vice president of marketing, and I truly believe that the marketing effort and her leadership are what have driven that company's growth.

MARKETING AND SALES ALIGNMENT

With your marketing goals and KPIs now established, it is time to start building rapport with your sales team members. In most circumstances, sales leaders and salespeople have defined sales targets, illustrated by one or more of the following:

1. Percent revenue increase
2. Number of new customers
3. Sales revenue target ($$$)

Any salesperson will tell you that these targets usually increase year over year and are harder and harder to achieve. If your company is like most other manufacturers, your sales team has not experienced a marketing department that has helped them meet their targets, so they may be a bit skeptical. Your goal in meeting with the sales leadership is to educate them on how marketing can help fill their sales funnel and to document what their goals are so that your future marketing plan is aligned to support them.

Why is this important?

The only way to truly measure marketing ROI is to be able to track closed sales revenue from the marketing effort (leads generated). You will need a strong relationship with your sales team for this. Earlier, I stated that if sales is the lifeblood of the company, then marketing is the blood pressure. They go hand in hand. Think of marketing as pre-sales. Your efforts should pave the way for sales success, and you deserve to take credit where credit is due.

Sales Goal = $$$$.

Once you have your sales team's goal defined, you can use it to ensure your marketing plan is in alignment.

In this chapter, you have learned all about goals, KPIs, and industry benchmarks and how they are the baseline requirements for an ROI-Driven Marketing Operation. You also learned what SMART goals are and how to differentiate between vanity metrics and key performance indicators. We covered how to begin building a relationship with your sales team for future collaboration. Perhaps most importantly, you now have a solid understanding of whether your marketing operation is a profit center or an expense to your company.

GOLD STANDARDS

Now that you understand the importance of goals, KPIs, and industry benchmarks in achieving a 10X ROI, it's time to begin making the changes that will set you on the road to success. Start by answering the following questions to assess your status and where you need to go:

1. Are your marketing goals defined and documented in writing, and are they ROI-driven?
2. Are your marketing goals specific, measurable, attainable, realistic, and timely (SMART)?
3. Do you have key performance indicators that align to your SMART goals?
4. Are you tracking marketing-generated leads from the first point of contact to closed new revenue or sales (HubSpot or integrated CRM)?
5. Are you regularly tracking lead quantity and quality?
6. Do you have a single source for marketing metrics and dashboards set up incorporating the most valuable KPIs pulled from various sources such as Google Analytics, Google AdWords, and marketing automation?
7. Are your report metrics agreed to by sales and marketing leadership?
8. Is your reporting completed weekly, semi-monthly, or monthly?

If you answered yes to at least six of these questions, congratulations! You are well on your way to having an ROI-Driven Marketing Operation. If you answered no to three or more questions, this is the place for you to begin work. At this point, it is likely that you are feeling overwhelmed with the tasks ahead of you. Most people answering these eight questions will have answered no to most of them. Don't be discouraged. You are starting on a journey to build a marketing operation that will not only help your company to scale (while positioning you as the hero) but also eliminate many of your sleepless nights due to your current marketing approach. Take one step at a time, and remember to measure your success based on how far you travel versus how far away you are from the end.

SEVEN: PILLAR 2

VALUE PROPOSITION, MESSAGING, AND BRANDING

W hen writing this book, we debated about which pillar was the most important for achieving ROI from marketing spend. The truth is that every pillar is critical in the equation. With that being said, I can't stress enough the importance of your value proposition and how you message and brand it.

This chapter focuses on developing a well-articulated and differentiated value proposition. The messaging and branding components are far too nuanced and detailed to outline in this book; however, we have provided some resources for your messaging and branding initiatives.

Time and time again, we have seen companies with great sales processes and strong marketing utterly fail at driving new business revenues due to a poorly articulated value proposition and the messaging and branding to support it. The reason? If buyers cannot connect with how your product or service will help them solve their problems or grow, they'll move on to find someone who can meet their expectations.

KEY DEFINITIONS

As we dive into this chapter, it's important to define the differences between a value proposition, messaging, and branding. While they all go together as one comprehensive unit, they are three separate components to your ROI-driven marketing strategy.

- **Value Proposition**: A value proposition is a clear statement that describes the benefit of your offer, how you solve your customer's problems, and what distinguishes you from the competition. It is the answer to one question: "If I am your ideal prospective customer, why should I buy from you rather than your competitors?"

- **Messaging**: Messaging is how you convey your value proposition through all your sales and marketing communications. Typically, this is done through the written word, either graphically or verbally.

- **Branding**: Branding is a huge topic in and of itself. For the purposes of this book, branding is the visual communication of your brand, including your logo, brand colors, fonts, and choice of imagery and how you present your message.

HOW B2B MANUFACTURING BUYERS MAKE BUYING DECISIONS

When your buyers make a buying decision, they often rely on a gut feeling based on one or more interactions with your manufacturing organization. These interactions can be as simple as meeting one of your employees, walking your shop floor, visiting your website, or using your phone answering system. Interactions can also be as complex as your product quality, customer service reputation, or pricing strategy. If a buyer feels secure and confident, their decision becomes easier.

To access the mind of your customer, get out a pen and paper, and write down a recent business purchase you made. This may have been hiring a contractor, or perhaps you purchased new software or hired an employee. Next, write down every reason you bought what you bought.

- Did you feel secure about your decision? Why?
- Were you confident that the person, product, or service solved your problem or met your aspirations? Why?
- What specifically helped you make that decision?
  - Positive reviews, testimonials, or references
  - Specific attributes (speed, quality, expertise, cost)
  - Professionalism in brand
  - Strong customer service
  - Equipment or area of specialization
  - Questions the seller answered
  - Effective website

Usually, a buying decision comes down to the value proposition, messaging, and branding of a product or service and how these three elements are presented to the buyer. If one of these elements is off, it sends signals to the buyer that something is not quite right, and security and confidence wane. When security and confidence wane, so do your chances of earning their business.

Today, B2B buyers are more educated than ever before. With so much information at their fingertips, most buyers have a multitude of choices when selecting a vendor, supplier, or service provider that clearly meets their time, quality, and price expectations. Great service, industry experience, high quality, and competitive pricing are required to enter the marketplace. They are not the tenets of a value proposition. The tenets of a strong value proposition comprise the following:

1. **Clarity**: Is your value clearly expressed in simple terms?
2. **Uniqueness**: Is your proposition differentiated among your competitors?
3. **Proof**: Can you provide proof to support your claims?
4. **The Why**: Does your value proposition illustrate why you are better than the competition?

It's very important to understand the framework we are building here. If you look on the internet, there are many differing definitions of what a value proposition is. A value proposition is also often confused with a unique selling proposition (USP). For the purposes of ROI-driven marketing, the value proposition is a framework of assets you must gather to craft a messaging strategy that will differentiate your company from your competitors, leading to increased sales. This chapter will walk you through the process.

Identifying the value you deliver throughout the buyer's journey is critical. B2B manufacturing buyers typically go through a four-step process when making a buying decision:

1. **Research of Their Options**: In this stage, buyers are doing research and looking for answers. Buyers in research mode want to be educated, advised, and informed regarding their options.

2. **Engagement with Potential Sellers**: When a buyer engages with a vendor or supplier, it's because they have a certain level of trust with the seller. However, they are still reviewing their options while becoming more educated. They are diving deeper into the funnel.

3. **Consideration and Evaluation of Sellers Who Meet Their Criteria**: At this point, buyers have narrowed down their choices to a small handful of sellers and are not very far from making a purchase.

4. **Commitment or Contract with a Specific Seller**: The buyer has made a commitment to purchase via a purchase order or contract.

This four-step process can take years or minutes, depending on the sale. If your value proposition, messaging, and branding are not strong, even if you have great marketing, you won't make it to Step 2! To make sure that your company is in the best position to make a sale, consider each of the following elements:

- **Research**: When buyers are doing their research, your company, product, or service must stand out. There are usually dozens of competitors looking to earn that buyer engagement. Does your value proposition stand out? Is it differentiated? Does it clearly illustrate how you solve your buyer's needs?

- **Engagement**: When a buyer engages with your company, it's because they saw or experienced something that made them think you can solve their problem or meet their aspiration. Is your value proposition reiterated and communicated in all your marketing communications?

- **Consideration and Evaluation**: At this step, it's likely the buyer's quality, time, and price needs are going to be met. What does your value proposition say to get you on the short list of companies they're considering? Now that you're on the short list of qualified providers, is your value proposition strong enough to win you the job? Can you back up your claims?

- **Confirmation**: Congratulations! You won the job! Is your value proposition strong enough to keep the customer over the long term?

Having a strong value proposition that resonates with your buyer during their buying process will result in more sales. Period. Failure to illustrate the value at any stage of the buyer's journey will likely mean that the buyer will go else-where. My experience has shown that most companies never consider the buyer's journey when crafting sales and marketing strategies. This is a big mistake! Years ago, the seller was in control of the sales process. The salesperson controlled what information was shared about your company and when. Today, the buyer controls the buying process, as most information they need is readily available on the internet. You must understand your buyer and how they make buying decisions. More on this later in the marketing strategy chapter.

DON'T FIX SYMPTOMS. FIX THE ROOT ISSUE.

A common scenario: your company recently launched an awesome new website. Social media, paid advertising, and email campaigns are underway. You have developed outreach lists and updated marketing collateral. Your sales team is making calls and attending industry events and trade shows. You can feel the buzz. It's exciting. All the hard work on strategy and planning is coming to fruition.

Months go by, and something is not right. Sales are not coming in. The website is not delivering quality leads. Salespeople are not closing new deals. You are confused and frustrated. Your company spent tens or perhaps hundreds of thousands of dollars on an enhanced sales and marketing infrastructure, and nothing has changed in the results column.

Executive leadership is starting to ask difficult questions. Shit is about to hit the fan.

The situation outlined above is not uncommon. The problem is that leadership usually doesn't fix the root issue because they don't know how to trace the symptoms back to the cause. Many business leaders and owners are used to fixing problems, so when their goal for growth isn't achieved, the first thing they do is look to fix their sales or marketing teams—and sometimes both. What happens next? Salespeople are replaced. Marketing team members or agencies are "fired," and new processes and technologies are embraced. Sometimes this works, but often the only thing that's fixed is the symptom, not the problem. Fast-forward eighteen months, and it's common for the same problems to persist; corporate growth was never achieved, and a lot of time and money were wasted.

To achieve the desired results, executives will

demand *more* marketing tactics, *more* sales outreach, *more* burnout, *more* turnover. *More* headaches.

This exact thing happened to us when working for one of our clients, a member-based bulk-purchasing organization for manufacturing firms. Seven months after engaging with them, two team members and I traveled to their headquarters for a face-to-face meeting with their leadership team.

We were very excited for this meeting. Leads were pouring in, and all the marketing metrics were above expectations. We brought all kinds of supporting documentation, analytics, and reports to show we were doing a great job.

We sat down in the conference room with approximately twelve others. Everyone was in a good mood. We were catching up and making small talk. We were confident, maybe even a little bit cocky.

Just before the meeting started, the president of the company, Samantha, walked in. Her body language was rigid and communicated she was not happy. She looked right at me and asked a pointed question: "Chris, we have only landed a handful of new members, and I expected a lot more by now. I am very disappointed with the results. What is going on?"

Admittedly, I was taken aback. In a panic, I quickly looked at Adam, the vice president of sales, hoping for support. Adam and I had a great rapport, and my understanding was that everyone was happy with the relationship.

Adam responded to Samantha, which gave me some extra time to think, but the question was mine to own. I knew marketing was driving the lead quality and quantity, and I knew Adam's team was feverishly working those leads. Their CRM (HubSpot) proved this. It was not a sales issue or a marketing issue. It had to be their value proposition. So I responded.

"Samantha, at the beginning of our relationship, I stated that within six to nine months, our methodology and systems would be able to identify whether you had a marketing issue, a sales issue, or a value proposition issue. I can say with confidence that marketing and sales are doing a great job. The data supports these claims. It must be a value proposition issue."

I then went on to share the data supporting our work and began to share my concerns for their value proposition. In all honesty, I had always had concerns about their value proposition but did not have the courage to bring it up. I didn't feel it was my place to speak up. After all, the issues affecting their membership acquisition (sales) were not necessarily marketing issues; they were operations issues. These issues were related to pricing of services, member onboarding, and member requirements.

It was a difficult meeting and a hard-learned lesson. We missed a critical component in go-to-market strategy. We should have addressed the client's value proposition early in our engagement.

Years later, Adam told me that Samantha was very unhappy with me after that meeting. I essentially called her "baby" ugly. However, we did fix the value proposition issue. The result was seventeen new members in the following three months—a new onboarding record. A year later, Samantha sold her company for top dollar to a larger competitor (who also became a client!).

CRAFTING A WELL-ARTICULATED AND DIFFERENTIATED VALUE PROPOSITION

Your company's value proposition is perhaps the number-one asset in your sales and marketing growth equation, yet so many companies fail to define one. Why? Listed below are the top five reasons:

1. It's hard work, and you have to dig deep.
2. Many executives underestimate the value.
3. You have to get executive leadership to buy into the process.
4. Many marketers have never built a value proposition and don't know where to start.
5. Many companies discover they are not different or what they think makes them unique really doesn't (this is the number-one reason).

Regardless of why your company has not defined a value proposition, if you follow the process outlined below, you can build a well-articulated and differentiated value proposition that will crush your competition.

Step 1: Ideal Customer Profile and Buyer Personas

Prior to developing value proposition messaging, we must first lay the basic groundwork upon which the value proposition stands. There are two foundational elements that must be defined first:

1. Your ideal customer profile
2. Buyer personas

Some people may argue that you should develop your value proposition first and then define the ideal customer profile and buyer personas, but I disagree. You must know who you are targeting before crafting messaging. When you go fishing, you don't start by purchasing a lure and let that determine what fish you are going to fish for; you start with the species of fish and then build a plan around how to attract and catch that fish. More on this below. For now, let's dive into the ideal customer profile (ICP).

The exercise included herein is intentionally designed to be basic to set the playing field. When building a marketing strategy, you may dive much deeper into detailed characteristics and buying motivations for your ICP and buyer personas.

Defining Your ICP

When anglers go fishing, they don't just go out to catch any type of fish. They go out targeting a specific species. This allows them to define a fishing strategy including the right lures, rods, reels, and tools. By targeting a specific species, the angler can make strategic decisions on which bodies of water to fish and which parts of each body of water will hold those fish. Any other approach would likely end in failure. This is why it's important to determine which type of fish (i.e., target customer) you want to catch before you go fishing (i.e., sales and marketing). To do this, answer the following questions and get your executive leadership to sign off. Visit our website at *www.G8P.co* to download our 10X ROI-Driven ICP Development Template.

- What is the ideal customer profile for your business? (Think of the ICP at the company level, not the person.)
- What industry or industries are they in?
- What is the size of their business (revenues or employees)?
- Where are they located (regional, national, international)?
- What problems do you solve for them?
- What are the unique characteristics of the customer company?

An example of my company's ideal customer profile is provided below:

- Manufacturing company with $50–$750 million in revenues
- Located in the United States
- Looking to aggressively scale and grow
- Private equity backed or owned
- Has implemented HubSpot or is considering HubSpot for marketing and sales software
- Has a marketing team that is looking to improve their metrics and is not delivering an ROI
- Specific manufacturing expertise in metals, chemicals, machinery, fabrication, textiles, plastic and rubber, heavy equipment, or electronics

Defining Your Buyer Personas

Leveraging your ICP, now think about the individual human beings who make buying decisions at these companies. We recommend starting with one to three buyer personas.

1. What is their role as it relates to buying products or services like yours? (We use "role," as the person's title may vary widely across your ICP target.)
2. What are they looking to accomplish, solve, or remedy?
3. Create a stereotype. What do you know about them?

4. How do they make buying decisions? What do they care about?

Step 2: Collection of Inputs

Now that your ICP and buyer personas are drafted, you are ready to build your value proposition. Gather a small team of diverse thinkers from your organization. Try to include a mix of those who work directly with the customer and those who can also see the big picture. Typically, this group is composed of five to seven people representing sales, customer service, executive leadership, and marketing. Ask what the customers really care about and what they are really buying. Remember, there is more to it than price, timing, quality, and customer service. You have to go deep and ask hard questions:

- What do you really sell to these buyers (e.g., a widget or peace of mind)?
- What do your buyers really want? What are they aspiring to achieve?
- What are the benefits of using your product or service versus those of competitors?
- What makes your product or service unique or different?

What do your buyers care about when making a buying decision? Look at it through their eyes. Pair up with your team, and talk about the business case issues and emotions that customers care about.

According to Miller Heiman Group/Korn Ferry, most buyers are looking to fix, accomplish, or avoid something, and they make their buying decision with that in mind. They do this considering two perspectives: what's in it for the business (i.e., business objectives), and what's in it for me personally (i.e., buyer emotions). Business and personal objectives may include one or more of the following:

Business Objectives	Buyer Emotions/Personal Goals
• Minimize	• Minimize
• Investment	• Fear and uncertainty
• Time	• Stress
• Risk	• Working hours
• Maximize	• Change
• Return on investment	• Failure/shame
• Speed	• Maximize
• Quality	• Pride
• Reliability	• Accomplishment
• Growth	• Prestige/promotion
	• Happiness
	• Simplicity
	• Work–life balance

Often, buyers make a purchase based on a gut feeling. This gut feeling is often influenced by an emotion, desire, or feeling. By understanding both the business's needs and the personal motivations of your buyers, you can craft your messaging to speak directly to your buyer to elicit these emotions, desires, or feelings. Usually, the buyer's attraction to a company or product is subconscious. Something in your marketing, branding, and messaging struck them as sticky. If your value proposition hits on one of their personal needs while fulfilling their company's needs, it makes doing business with you more appealing.

Step 3: Unique Features and Characteristics

In Step 3, you'll build out a list of unique features and characteristics of your organization. Then you'll ask your team two questions:

1. So what?
2. Can we prove it's true?

Try to come up with at least three to four unique characteristics. For example, your company might have a trademarked process or software. You might operate within an industry, product, or service niche. Your service might include a particular specialty or feature. Or you might be better, faster, stronger, or cheaper than your competitors. If you have more than four, document all of them.

Often, there is not one unique characteristic that truly differentiates you from your competitors. It is usually a combination of characteristics that creates differentiation.

The most powerful value propositions are supported by data or proof while resonating with the buyer's needs. Once you have your list of unique characteristics, ask yourself, "So what?" Why would your buyers care about each unique characteristic? Do the characteristics, whether combined or singular, resonate with your buyer based on their needs and their company's needs in relation to your offering?

The next question is what proof can you provide to support why buyers should choose you?

Examples of proof:

- Certifications
- Demonstrated expertise (case studies, customer testimonials, or reviews)
- Documented results (metrics/data)
- Awards

Now fill in the blanks using the following statement:

We are confident that customers will buy from us because our company solves [insert customer problem(s)] better than any alternative because:

- *Proof 1:* _____
- *Proof 2:* _____
- *Proof 3:* _____

Step 4: Marketing Language

With the same group of thinkers in the room, start to formulate your value proposition statements. You can do this on a whiteboard or onscreen. Consider your inputs, along with your unique features and characteristics. You should do more than one and then take a step back.

Write down three to five sentences that clearly illustrate the following:

- Who your ICP is
- What problems you solve for them
- How you are unique
- What proof you can provide to back up your claims

Once you've generated your sentences, evaluate the merit of each one:

- Is it clear and easily understood?
- Is it believable?
- Does it show how you are different?
- Does it state the value you offer?
- Is it backed up with proof?

Step 5: Value-Added "Backers"

Now that you have your value proposition foundation, consider your value-added backers. These are the everyday things you take for granted that can back up what you say your offering can do for your customers. Many times, you are in a highly competitive market, and the little things can sway a customer in your favor. Make a list of the backers that support your value proposition.

Examples of value-added backers:

- Free consulting
- Transparency in pricing
- Guarantees
- Trademarked processes

- Unique customization
- Industry associations and partners

Value-added backers are different from proof points in that these are typically "extras" that a buyer will get when doing business with you, whereas proof points demonstrate your past ability to deliver the value you state.

Step 6: Finalization and Testing

At this point, you should have the tenets of a well-articulated and differentiated value proposition. It is up to you to craft how this value proposition is leveraged throughout all of your marketing and sales communications.

The best way to tell whether your value proposition message is strong is to test it. You can easily do this on your website or via social media. We call this A/B testing. It's a technique we use to validate your marketing messages. It also helps you make data-based decisions when you finalize your value proposition.

In an A/B test of your value proposition message, you take a webpage or an app screen and modify it to create a second version of the same page. Half of your traffic is shown one value proposition message, and the other half is shown another version of your value proposition message. Their engagement with each value proposition is measured and collected using analytical tools. The results should suggest which value proposition you should more strongly consider.

WHAT TO DO IF YOU ARE NOT UNIQUE

The reason companies don't often have strong value propositions is a lack of differentiation in the marketplace. It is not uncommon to go through the above exercises and realize that your organization is not as differentiated or unique as you had hoped. This can be a frustrating realization.

About fifteen years ago, I took my company, SyncShow, through the above exercise, and upon completion, we realized we were not all that different from other marketing agencies. We did work for anyone who paid us, and there was nothing really unique about us. We did good work. Clients were happy and referring business, but we weren't unique. It was a bit deflating.

The good news is that we saw an opportunity for the future. We buckled down and evaluated our competition. We realized that many of our competitors were not all that different either. So we began a journey to become unique. Over the following months and years, we focused our efforts to develop a well-articulated and differentiated value proposition.

We first refined our niche to only business-to-business companies, with manufacturing as our primary market. We further narrowed our niche to online marketing rather than being a full-service marketing agency. We focused on being HubSpot experts. We built proprietary processes and trademarked them. We then focused on being an ROI-driven marketing consulting and implementation firm. The result: we are now very unique, and our value proposition and messaging illustrate this.

In this chapter, you have learned how to craft a well-articulated and differentiated value proposition. From my experience, this is the hardest part of the ROI-Driven Marketing Operation. Teaming up with your sales team and executive leadership can open a Pandora's box of conversations, arguments, and differing opinions. It is for this reason that many companies skip this critical step. If you find the value proposition process is difficult, don't quit! When it gets challenging, and it will, you are on the right track. Keep at it, and dig deep.

Sometimes companies discover that they are not unique at all. If this is the case, develop a plan for how you can become unique, and in the meantime, do the best you can with what you have. Work to continually improve, improvise, adapt, and overcome.

Solving great problems brings great value and success.

GOLD STANDARDS

To determine whether your value proposition is at its most effective, consider the following questions:

1. Is your value proposition messaging simple, clear, and to the point?
2. Do you have a straightforward value proposition, clearly presented on your website, stating what you do, who you do it for, and why it matters to your buyer?
3. Does your value proposition clearly illustrate the problems you solve for your customers or clients?

4. Does your website content clearly showcase proof points to validate your value proposition claims?

5. Is the messaging of your value proposition consistent throughout all your marketing and sales collateral, including social media accounts?

6. Does your website home page showcase a formal process to doing business with your organization?

7. Do you have established brand standards for logo use, design, and fonts?

8. Do you have an established brand voice for your company that is utilized for all written, video, and audio marketing and sales communications?

9. Do you have an ideal customer profile with documented characteristics?

10. Do your corporate and product logos accurately represent a professional image?

If you answered yes to at least eight of these questions, congratulations! You are well on your way to having a strong value proposition, messaging, and branding footprint.

If you answered no to three or more questions, it's time to get working on your value proposition. This is one of the most important aspects of your ROI-driven marketing campaign.

MARKETING STRATEGY

Having worked with hundreds of manufacturing companies over a twenty-year period, we found that not one was able to provide us with an existing written marketing strategy—not one. It's no wonder that so many marketers struggle to attain the results they are striving for. A marketing department with a formal strategy is a marketing department that reaches its goals!

For ROI-driven marketing, your marketing strategy should be a formal written document and include multi-channel strategies for *inbound marketing* and *outbound marketing.* How much of each will be based on your specific goals, budget, and time frames.

Often, we'll talk to prospects who say that digital marketing hasn't worked for them in the past and that it's "a waste of time and money and provides no real return on investment." This objection was the foundation for the development of the Great 8 Pillars methodology—to prove that digital marketing can provide a significant ROI and contribute to your organization's scale objectives.

So when prospects tell us digital marketing hasn't worked, what they really mean is they haven't done it the right way or they've toed into certain areas but haven't embraced a full-scale strategic and multichannel approach.

To be blunt, this is the company that spends tens or hundreds of thousands of dollars on marketing with no defined marketing strategy. It's the company that builds a website and thinks it's going to be like *The Field of Dreams—if you build it, they will come.* It's the company that blasts out email newsletters when the mood strikes to a list of cobbled-together customers, trade show prospects, and names on business cards from the bottoms of their desk drawers.

A best-in-class digital marketing strategy should be approached as an integrated inbound and outbound marketing strategy. In order to drive a 10X ROI, you need strategic planning in each area, so let's break them down.

- **Inbound Marketing**: Inbound marketing is the art of allowing prospects and customers to find your brand as they're going through their independent buyer's journey. It's all about attraction. The concept is built on the foundation of creating customer-centric content that speaks to buyer pain points and encourages prospects to make a buying decision proactively—inviting your sales team to have a seat at the table. Inbound marketing is all about being found by buyers when they are doing their research, the first stage in their buyer's journey. Common tactics and strategies for inbound marketing include search engine optimization, content marketing (video, blogging, and thought leadership), specific types of email marketing, and social media.

- **Outbound Marketing**: Sometimes it's easier to understand what something is by knowing what it's not. Inbound marketing is the opposite of outbound marketing. Inbound marketing encourages your buyers to invite your sales teams to have a seat at the table. Outbound marketing typically interrupts your buyer during their day. It's marketing that hits buyers when they are not expecting it, such as email marketing, advertising, direct mail, and some social media tactics. When done poorly, it can irritate your buyers. When done properly, it can generate strong results.

Effective ROI-driven marketing incorporates aspects of both inbound and outbound marketing. By combining both baiting (attraction/inbound) and hunting (interruption/outbound), you spread a wider net, leading to a greater sales pipeline and lead flow.

BUILDING YOUR MARKETING STRATEGY

Now that you understand the importance of having a formal marketing strategy, it's time to start crafting one. Let's start with the basics.

Your marketing strategy is a trickle-down system of processes. If you follow the processes from top to bottom, the system will work. The good news is that you have already completed several steps in the system. Below is an outline of each of everything involved in building an ROI-driven marketing strategic plan:

1. Define a three-year vision for marketing objectives
2. Develop ROI-driven goals
3. Key performance indicators
4. Your ideal customer profile (ICP)
5. Your buyer personas and correlating buyer journeys
6. Search engine optimization strategy
7. Social media strategy
8. Content marketing strategy
9. Conversion strategy
10. Inbound marketing strategy
11. Outbound marketing strategy
12. Twelve-month marketing calendar and rollout plan

These twelve components should also be the table of contents of your marketing strategy document. Visit our website at *www.G8P.co* to download our 10X ROI-Driven Marketing Strategy Template. This is the same template we use for our clients.

Before you begin, please note that the focus of this chapter is to assist you in crafting a formal written marketing strategy, not explain how to do marketing. Certain sections of this chapter provide general guidelines to steer you in the right direction. With today's marketing best practices changing daily, it is your job to keep up with the trends and fill in the blanks. Also worth noting is that your written strategy may not include all twelve sections. For example, you may wish to focus on inbound marketing instead of outbound marketing. Your strategy should fit your organization's needs, and it's up to you to define those needs.

To complete the template, address each section as follows.

Three-Year Vision for Marketing Objectives

Your three-year vision can be very simple or complex. It should be a documented outline of your future vision for marketing. At my company, SyncShow, we keep this pretty simple, with one to four paragraphs or bullet points of the key marketing objectives for the future, usually thirty-six months out. To write your three-year vision, ask yourself the following questions:

- What are your marketing priorities over the next six to twelve months?
- What will get in the way of your success?
- What components of your marketing strategy are important but not critical right now?

- What will drive the most marketing value to your organization today versus in the future?
- What is your organization doing well in marketing now versus what needs to be improved? (The Diagnostic and Roadmap will help you with this.)

Three-Year Vision

YEAR 1
- Implement key Great 8 Pillars golden standards
- Value proposition refinement and coordinating branding and messaging
- Focus on lead generation by implementing multiple paid campaigns like PPC, paid LinkedIn and programmatic ads
- Reverse negative trends on your website via technical improvements, SEO, content development
- Improve the sales process to better keep leads warm through lead nurturing emails
- Create a practice of continuous improvement by identifying CRO and A/B test to improve conversion rate
- Establish new benchmark KPIs, based on increased marketing efforts

YEAR 2
- Implement and refine key Great 8 Pillars golden standards
- Introduce account-based marking (ABM) to attract larger high-profile ICPs
- Improve digital product-based assets via sales materials, and chatbot guiding prospects to the right products and services
- Rebuild website aligned with your value proposition and highlighting benefits to key industries
- Revisit sales pipeline timing and CRM alignment to identify opportunities to improve close rate

YEAR 3
- Implement and refine key Great 8 Pillars golden standards
- Develop fully coordinated sales and marketing plan based on shared revenue goals
- Create specific content and goals for each pipeline stage enabling you to better understand revenue opportunity and performance
- Build off-site SEO presence by partnering with select agencies and thought leaders in the safety space for content opportunities
- Refine sales collateral for improved ROI

- What does the organization have in the marketing budget this year versus future years?

Once you have answered these questions, you are ready to draft your three-year vision for marketing objectives. Remember to keep it simple; these objectives will most likely change as the future brings more information. See the example of a three-year vision.

ROI-Driven Goals

Insert your ROI goals as defined in Chapter 6.

Supporting Key Performance Indicators

Insert your KPIs as defined in Chapter 6.

Your Ideal Customer Profile (ICP)

As we discussed in Chapter 7, an ICP is a defined set of characteristics held by organizations that will get the most value from your product/service offering and, therefore, the type of organization that will drive the most revenue growth for your company.

Having an ICP also helps you save time and money by focusing sales and marketing efforts on the greatest value opportunities. To use the fishing analogy again, it is akin to fishing with a spear instead of a net. Most companies we work with do not have the budget to go after multiple markets, and spreading your marketing budget over multiple ICPs can water down effectiveness. Remember, it's all about outcomes over output.

Here's how we are going to help you define your perfect ICP. The easiest way to get started is to download the Great 8 ICP Development Template from our website at *www.G8P.co.* You can also follow the instructions below:

Step 1: Executive Alignment Meeting

Don't do this alone. Although this exercise can be easily completed by marketing, we recommend that you reach out to the executive leadership of your company or division and get their input on each of the following steps.

Schedule a meeting with your leadership team, including the highest-ranking sales leader. The objective of the meeting is to review the ICP template together and come to a mutual agreement on who your ICP is, including your best customers and defining characteristics as outlined below. You may even want to send them the Great 8 ICP Development Template to fill out in advance. Doing so will save a lot of time and rework.

STEP 1A: BEST CUSTOMERS

Write down a list of the best customers you serve. These should be the companies that you like to work with the most, bring in the most money, and get the most value from your product or service. Your list should include somewhere between three and ten current or past customers.

STEP 1B: DEFINING CHARACTERISTICS

You can gather ideal customer characteristics from your marketing, sales, or customer support teams. You should consider each of the companies you listed in Step 2 when making a characteristics list. There's a good chance that you will need to reach out to your clients directly for some of the information. The more specific you get, the better. Dive deep, and really challenge yourself. Consider the following elements:

- **Company Revenue**: How big or small is your ideal client in annual sales revenue?
- **Timing**: Is there a time of year when purchasing decisions are made for your product or service at these companies?
- **Industry**: Many industry verticals have sub-verticals, such as manufacturing > textiles >

construction fabrics. Get as specific as you can.

- **Company Size**: How many employees work there?
- **Team Size**: Are you selling a product or service to a specific department? How big is their team? Does the size of this team factor into your targeting?
- **Geography**: Where are these companies located? Within a two-hundred-mile radius of your offices? National? Global?
- **Budget**: How much are they spending on your product or service?
- **Knowledge of Your Product/Service**: How much does the company know about your industry, product, or service? Does this matter in targeting?
- **Business Objectives**: Does your product or service contribute to their business objectives?
- **Growth Stage**: Are they in a startup, growth, mature, or decline stage?
- **Lagging or Succeeding**: Are they in pain or growth mode?
- **Challenges**: What issues did they face before purchasing your product or service?
- **Differentiators**: Why do they typically choose your company over competitors (price, technology, people, guarantees, process)?

- **Precipitating Factors**: Are there certain factors that make these companies more likely to do business with you (merger, acquisition, funding, product recall)?
- **Other**: The list goes on. There are many more characteristics that your ideal customers may have, so if there's something else that you would like to include, be sure to add it.

Step 2: Vetting the Profile

With this information, you are now getting closer to having an ICP. As you review the characteristics of your ideal customer profile, the objective is to focus, refine, and focus again. The more specific and targeted, the better. Home in as much as you can.

Run your profile past executive leadership at all levels. This is a must. You'd be surprised at how many times I have seen the marketing and sales teams develop an ICP that the president or CEO disagrees with. Alignment and buy-in from all stakeholders is key.

Congratulations! By now you should have a final ideal customer profile. Remember to update the profile as knowledge is gained or the ideal changes. You are on your way to crafting enhanced marketing strategies for the organizations that need your product or service the most, and they will be your best customers to boot.

YOUR BUYER PERSONAS AND
CORRELATING BUYER JOURNEYS

Now that you have your ICP defined, we must identify and build individual profiles for those who make purchasing decisions within the ICP. As you'll recall from Chapter 7, we call these buyer personas. Provided on the following page is a simple graphic to illustrate a completed buyer persona.

There are a lot of templates available online for buyer persona development; however, we have found many miss the mark. They are too general and ask questions that have little impact on marketing and sales decisions. The easiest way to get started is to download the Great 8 Buyer Persona Development Template from our website at *G8P.co*. You can also follow the instructions below.

Your buyer persona is a semi-fictional depiction of the decision-makers within your ideal customer profile who will determine whether their organization uses your product or service. A good buyer persona outlines the specific needs, or pain points, of this person in relation to your product or service. When you start this process, it's best to

Ted

30-55 · Engineer

BACKGROUND
- Bachelor's or master's degree in engineering
- Spends his day working on blueprints, product drawings, and CAD files
- He evaluates procedures such as equipment design and the system performance involved with the manufacturing of a particular product
- Provides process and environment information to the buyer to ensure they are making an informed purchasing decision
- Focuses on the big picture and will pull in a specialist engineer when needed

IDENTIFIERS
- Detail-oriented
- Strong analytical skills
- Technical
- Wants to be seen as smart and a problem solver
- Actively researches equipment, solutions, or issues
- Tends to struggle with face-to-face communication skills
- Active on LinkedIn

OBJECTIONS
How do I know I can trust your product to be as efficient and reliable as you say it is? I need to choose the right equipment for my job and if I can't be sure this is right for my project, I won't work with you.

GOALS & OBJECTIVES
- Analyze how process changes will affect overall production and the product. Focus on continually improving project processes.
- Find solutions to product problems based on quality and performance
- Ensure long-term durability and product life span
- Monitor equipment to ensure maintenance tasks are carried out
- Perform risk assessments of equipment and processes not only for productivity, but also for safety of operation

PAIN POINTS
- Convincing the buyer to spend more money on a higher-quality product
- Aggressive timelines
- Convincing upper management that his ideas are valid and providing the company with results
- Technical service issues
- Works long hours

MARKETING MESSAGE
Our broad scope of equipment offerings and capabilities have made us the first choice for customers around the globe. Our equipment can help support your unique, complex, and rugged manufacturing needs while giving you the peace of mind that it will stand the test of time. Our data-driven, experienced sales team will come to you and provide personalized consultations based on your project's needs.

BUYER'S JOURNEY

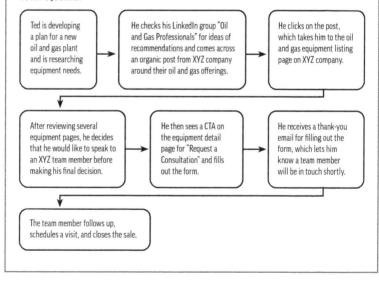

build a minimum of two to three buyer personas for each ICP that you have. This usually will consist of three types of people:

- **User**: This person uses or manages users of your product or service. This is often the person conducting research and looking for you or the person you want to reach out to.

- **Financial Leader**: This leader oversees purchasing decisions and return on investment.

- **Final Decision-Maker**: This could be a manager-level person or senior executive, depending on business size. Regardless, this is the person who ultimately has yes/no decision-making power.

It is very possible that your buyer does not fall into any of these roles. It's important to talk to your salespeople, current customers, and prospects to determine the roles of your buyer persona.

Start with accountabilities. A person's title within a company and their actual responsibilities can vary significantly from organization to organization. A general

manager, procurement manager, or engineer at one manufacturer may have different accountabilities than those
at another manufacturer. That's why it's important to
start with their specific accountabilities (i.e., what are
they responsible for?). For each buyer persona, you'll want
to make a list of the specific accountabilities within their
role to get a better idea of what they do.

Once you have their accountabilities defined, you can
list the titles they may hold—operations manager, project
manager, or safety manager—which may differ based on
the company. Many companies have different titles for
similar roles, so do your homework to list all titles.

After this, detail the following traits of this person (use
identifiers that matter for your company; not all of these
will be applicable):

1. **Age Range**: Helps determine messaging tone,
   brand voice, and where they may engage online
2. **Geographic Location**: Helps in targeting as well as
   choosing tactics for attracting and engaging
3. **Number of Years in the Company**: Typically
   important if your company targets new employees
   or employees who have just transitioned into a
   new role

4. **Number of Years in the Industry**: Indicates whether they are a mature buyer or new and learning
5. **Certifications Held**: Helps identify them based on specific certifications
6. **Gender**: Helps identify specific groups or associations a person may belong to and also helps craft your messaging appropriately

Then begin to outline the specific traits of this person. Consider, for example, the following:

1. **Technical Expertise**: General knowledge only or highly knowledgeable and detailed (on a scale of 1–10, with 10 being highest)
2. **Knowledge of Your Industry**: Level of knowledge regarding your product or service (on a scale of 1–10, with 10 being highest)
3. **Seniority in Organization**: Staff, manager, vice president, or C-suite
4. **Data-Driven**: To what level do they use data to make buying decisions? (On a scale of 1–10, with 10 being highest)
5. **Value-Driven**: To what level do they leverage value

in making buying decisions? (On a scale of 1–10, with 10 being highest)

6. **Risk Tolerance**: Do they make decisions with a very high degree of assessment, or do they take calculated risks? (On a scale of 1–10, with 10 being highest)

7. **Quality-Driven vs. Price-Driven**: Are they looking for high quality, or are they focused on value?

8. **Pain-Driven vs. Growth-Driven**: Are they looking to solve a problem or scale?

9. **Work-Life Balance**: 0 = work is life, 10 = only comes in the office a few days a week

To understand your buyer even more intimately, consider the following:

1. **Goals and Objectives**: List one to five goals and objectives each buyer has in regard to your product or service at their job/organization.

2. **Pain Points**: These are the headaches this person has to deal with day in, day out that drive them up the wall as related to your competitors' products or services. List one to five general pain points. If there are more, please list them.

3. **Specific Identifiers**: Identify as many hyper-specific traits as possible. Examples may include the following:
   a. Are they data-driven?
   b. Are they deadline-driven?
   c. How do they prefer to communicate with people (e.g., email, text message, phone, Slack)?
   d. Where do they consume information/media?
   e. What channels do they use (e.g., email, social media, industry associations)? Use your own analytics from past customers to see how they found your organization.
   f. Do they get their information from someone inside the organization? (If so, this person may be another buyer persona.)
   g. What industry or professional groups or associations do they belong to?

4. **Common Objections to Your Product or Service**: What are the common objections this person has to buying your product or service? How do you overcome these objections? Write out responses to each objection that will help overcome it.

Remember that it's important to use all the information you have on this individual. Think of the challenges they are facing. What are their goals? Use that information to wrap all that up into a response so powerful they would be crazy to say no.

After this, you can fill out the following template:

- **Give Them a Name**: This can be a basic name, or you can go with something a bit more descriptive. Many like to reference the specific role of the person (e.g., Executive Eric) so you know exactly who you're referring to.

- **Bio**: If you were to condense all the information you learned about this person into a paragraph, how would you do it? For a template, you can start out with the organization where they work (reference the ICP) and then discuss some of their responsibilities in that organization. After that, mention two or three of the most important traits that matter to this person.

- **Traits on a Scale of 1–10**: Insert a graph or a scale that can rate these traits on a scale of 1–10.

- **Goals and Objectives**: List their goals.

- **Pain Points**: List their pain points in relation to your industry.

- **Knowledge of Your Industry**: Provide a quick description of how well this person knows your industry, company, and product. This will be a super-helpful reference for marketing and sales teams, who will be able to use it to determine how they will communicate with this person.

- **Common Objections and Your Responses**: Build a table that has the common objections and the responses.

Visit our website at *www.G8P.co* to download our 10X ROI-Driven Buyer Persona Template.

ALIGNMENT IS EVERYTHING

Years ago, we had a client that hired us to complete a strategy session. We entered the conference room, and the CEO had arrived early and was sitting at the table. He asked me what the Ideal Customer Profile exercise encompassed. I told him it was the exercise to document his company's target buyer or customer for marketing attraction purposes.

He stated, "That's easy—we service billion-dollar tier-one and two suppliers to the automotive industry."

Two hours later, we finished our exercise, and seven of his leadership team members built out the company's ICP. Not one executive had billion-dollar tier-one or two suppliers on the list. The CEO was confused and embarrassed that he and his team were not on the same page. He had lost touch with his organizational direction.

Make sure you involve multiple stakeholders when building out your ICP and buyer personas!

Search Engine Optimization Strategy

Search engine optimization (SEO) is a critical component of your overall marketing strategy. It filters through multiple components of your plan, including your social media strategy, content strategy, outbound and inbound marketing strategies, and website. It is for this reason that we include it as a separate component of your strategic documentation.

Search engine optimization is a rapidly changing component of marketing. The tools, tactics, and best practices are always in flux. Consequently, we do not provide you with a detailed, step-by-step outline of how to complete this part of your marketing strategy.

- Current-state SEO SWOT (strengths, weaknesses, opportunities, and threats) analysis
- SEO keyword research and listing
- SEO competitive analysis

Your goal in this section is to ensure you have a solid search engine optimization plan built on data, not guesswork. You may need to contact an agency or freelancer that specializes in SEO to complete this section. Specialty software and deep SEO knowledge are musts. Do your homework, and draft a plan. Then watch the results come in.

Ask yourself these questions to get started:

- What is your current SEO status?
    - What are you ranking for now? Do you want to be ranking for these terms?
    - What should you be ranking for?
- What keywords does your target buyer incorporate into their online search queries when looking for your product or services?
- What do your competitors rank for? (Research at least three competitors.)
- Which competitors are stealing market share that you want to capitalize on? (Often, your competitors are not necessarily companies you are competing against directly. They may be companies that are stealing market share online, and you never actually go up against them. Do a keyword search to see which companies are dominating the results page.)
- What products or services do you need to drive sales for?
- Does your SEO strategy support your corporate growth goals?

KNOW YOUR ENEMY

One of our customers was a manufacturer of circuit boards. We were retained to build out their marketing strategy, and in the process, we completed an SEO competitor analysis. We ascertained their top three competitors and completed the analysis.

When doing our research, we found that none of the competitors ranked for their chosen search terms. They obviously were not stealing market share by garnering online traffic. However, one Chinese company dominated search engine rankings. We were able to find that this manufacturer was spending three times more money on search engine optimization and paid advertising than our client's whole marketing budget.

When we presented our findings to our customer, the president stated that this Chinese company was not a competitor that they went up against, even though they played in the same space. I stated that while this company may not be a direct competitor they were losing to on requests for proposals, the company was stealing business from them, as they dominated the online realm.

Be sure to research who your competitors really are!

Social Media Strategy

Do you have one? This is the big question that must be answered. If you do not have a social media strategy documented in writing, then you don't have one. Your goal in this section is to ensure you have a solid social media plan built on data, not guesswork.

Your social media strategy will filter through your inbound and outbound marketing strategies. We recommend you have at least two social media strategies, with one dedicated to inbound marketing (thought leadership and educational content) and one to outbound marketing (direct outreach to buyers).

Many companies use social media for culture, recruiting, and general public relations. This is great and should not be impeded. However, for ROI-driven marketing, your social media strategy must have ROI-driven goals. Ask yourself these questions when building your social media strategy:

- How can we use social media to improve revenues?

- How will social media support our ROI goals?
- Are we measuring social media effectiveness in our reporting?
- What data do we need from social media to define success?
- What social media platforms do our prospects and customers use?
- What business groups or industry associations do they belong to on social media?
- Where do our customers and prospects consume educational content, and how can we position ourselves as thought leaders?
- How can we leverage social media advertising and list development?

Once you have answered these questions, you can start to build out a formal social media strategy. Be sure to download our 10X ROI-Driven Marketing Strategy Template and reference our social media strategy section to help you in developing your content plan.

Content Marketing Strategy

Do you have one? You may be starting to see a theme here. If you do not have a content marketing strategy documented in writing, then you don't have one. Your goal in this section is to ensure you have a content marketing plan built on data, not guesswork.

Just like SEO and social media, your content marketing strategy will filter through your inbound and outbound marketing strategies. Ask yourself these questions when building your content marketing strategy:

- What types of content do our buyers prefer to consume (e.g., video, written, graphical, interactive)?
- Are we answering all of our buyer and customer questions throughout their buying journeys?
- What format of content will be represented in our content strategy (e.g., white papers, videos, case studies, articles, e-books, website content)?
- What content assets do we have that support buyer and customer needs throughout their buying journeys?
- Where should this content be published?
- Are search engine optimization keywords included in our content to assist in driving our SEO objectives?
- Do we have adequate content assets to prove our value proposition claims?

- Are we positioned as a thought leader, and if not, what do we need to do to become one?
- Do we have the appropriate amount and type of content assets to meet our marketing objectives?
- How will our content support our ROI goals?
- Are we measuring our content's effectiveness in our reporting?
- What data do we need from our content consumption to define success?

Once you have answered these questions, you can start to build out a formal content marketing strategy. Be sure to download our 10X ROI-Driven Marketing Strategy Template and reference our content marketing strategy section to help you in developing your content plan.

Conversion Strategy

Defining how you will convert engaged prospects and customers from being casual consumers of your marketing content into new customers and bigger customers must be part of your strategy. Many marketing teams and agencies don't properly plan for this component, and it's a big mistake.

Your conversion strategy should include documentation on your unique conversion stages and how you will progress buyers from one stage to the next until they become excluded or new customers. These stages are typically as follows:

General Contact > Lead > Marketing-Qualified Lead > Sales-Qualified Lead > Customer

Every tactical marketing implementation must have a conversion strategy associated with it. As an example, every blog article you post should have a strategy for enticing the reader to take the next step, whatever that step is. Every marketing email sent or paid advertisement placed must have a conversion strategy.

Additionally, buyers often need to be coddled over their buying journey (your sales cycle). This journey can last anywhere from a couple of days to several years. Your conversion strategy should include lead-nurturing and sales-support aspects to pull individuals through the life cycle stages.

It is important to address that this section of your strategic plan should not incorporate every tactical conversion strategy. Doing so would consume hundreds if not thousands of pages of documentation. However, what you do need to include is your overarching conversion rules or guidelines.

Ask yourself these questions when building your conversion strategy:

- How will you pull prospects and customers into your funnel and convert them to paying customers?
- How can you attain data to inform marketing and sales direction?
- What rules or standard operating procedures must be in place to enable conversion?
- What systems or software are required for conversion practices (e.g., HubSpot)?
- What key assets do you need to convert leads (e.g., landing pages, forms, databases, CRM, calls to action, graphics, content assets, email outreach)?
- What roles do sales and marketing play in conversion?
- When are lead-nurturing tactics implemented?

Once you have answered these questions, you can start to build out a formal conversion strategy. Be sure to download our 10X ROI-Driven Marketing Strategy Template and reference our conversion strategy section to help you in developing your conversion plan.

Inbound Marketing Strategy

Inbound marketing is typically the most time intensive to develop because it requires you to build out the components of your social media, content, conversion, and SEO strategies, so gaining traction here is going to take the most time. This can be a "slow to grow" area. It is for this reason that we recommend starting your inbound implementation first. It makes the most sense to give your team the greatest amount of running room possible. The good news is that once you launch the successful assets for this leg of your stool, you can leverage them in your outbound program. This helps to lighten your load and gives you an opportunity to repurpose the great work created by your team. A strong inbound marketing strategy allows your team to work smarter, not harder, so you can focus on outcomes versus output.

While components of an inbound marketing strategy may feel highly foundational, doing it correctly is crucial for setting up a campaign for success. So eat the frog—get it over with, and you'll thank us later.

Throughout this chapter, we have talked about integrated marketing disciplines—specifically search engine optimization, content marketing, conversion, and social media marketing. If you have followed the process, these individual strategies were based on your three-year vision, goals, ICP, and buyer personas. Now it is time to pull them together and build a plan for attraction.

To attract the attention of the right buyer, you must create valuable content that serves their needs—educates, informs, and, sometimes, if you're very funny or very clever, entertains. The goal of inbound marketing is to begin to develop trust as an authority for the problem they're trying to solve or the goal they are wishing to attain. The implementation of your strategy should be completely altruistic. It should not sell your services, and it should be objective; perhaps it even mentions and highlights your competitors to provide clarity and transparency to help the buyer align with what they want. At this stage, a buyer is simply weighing their options between what happens if they do something or nothing and seeing what that "something" includes.

Your inbound marketing strategy should document how you are going to attract prospective buyers to your brand leveraging the following:

- Your social media strategy
- Your search engine optimization strategy
- Your search engine marketing/advertising tactics

- Your content strategy and assets
- Your conversion strategy
- The positioning of your value proposition
- Your website

Don't overcomplicate your inbound marketing strategy. You have already built out the foundational elements in the previous sections of this book. Crafting a beautiful and extensive marketing strategy that you cannot implement would be a total waste of time. Remember, keep it simple. Develop a plan that works for you, and make it SMART (specific, measurable, attainable, realistic, and timely).

Ask yourself these questions when building your inbound marketing strategy:

- What elements of our content, social media, conversion, and SEO strategies are appropriate for an overarching inbound marketing strategy to attract buyers and position our organization as a thought leader?

- What are the most appropriate vehicles and channels I can leverage to get our brand in front of buyer personas at our ICP (e.g., associations, publications, social media, search engine)?

Once you have answered these questions, you can start to build out a formal inbound marketing strategy. Be sure to download our 10X ROI-Driven Marketing Strategy Template and reference our inbound marketing strategy section to help you in developing your inbound plan.

Outbound Marketing Strategy

Outbound marketing, when done correctly and as part of this three-legged-stool approach, can turn an average marketing plan into a highly robust one. The key to successful outbound marketing is to use what you've found to be successful in inbound marketing and leverage that for your outbound marketing. Ensure you have a bulletproof ideal customer profile and unique value proposition. Then leverage your key assets from inbound, and something that had momentum now has a lot of tentacles reaching folks through all the inbound marketing channels *plus* email marketing, advertising, direct social media, programmatic advertising, geotargeting, and 1:1 outreach.

Since so much outbound marketing is "hunting" focused, when done the right way, it's a fantastic way to quickly reach your sales-qualified lead and ROI goals. Ask yourself these questions when building your outbound marketing strategy:

- How can I "place" my organization's marketing messaging and assets in the hands of my target buyers?
- What channels or vehicles have been successful in the inbound marketing program that I can leverage for outbound?
- Where can I obtain a list of my ideal customer profile and coordinating buyer personas?
- How do I systematically hit those individuals on the list with integrated inbound and outbound marketing?
- If I interrupt a prospective buyer with my content, what will get them to "listen" to my message rather than the competition?
- How does my marketing stand out from the competition?

Once you have answered these questions, you can start to build a formal outbound marketing strategy. Be sure to download our 10X ROI-Driven Marketing Strategy Template and reference our outbound marketing strategy section to help you in developing your outbound plan.

Twelve-Month Marketing Calendar and Rollout Plan

Your marketing calendar and rollout plan comprise the visual outline of your implementation schedule. This is where you document when you will do what. Your calendar should illustrate the major milestones of your strategy.

At SyncShow, our marketing calendars and rollout plans take two forms. One is a high-level calendar view with key milestones and durations for the larger marketing initiatives. The second is a detailed project management plan that is built out in our project management system.

	Jan	Feb	Mar	Apr	May	Jun	Jul	Aug	Sep	Oct	Nov	Dec
Content Calendar	■											
Blogs, Social, and Email Blast		■		■		■		■		■		■
SEO Improvements	■	■	■	■	■	■	■	■	■	■	■	■
Presentation Branding	■	■	■									
CRO/Services Pages	■	■	■	■	■	■	■	■	■	■	■	■
Website Maintenance	■	■	■	■	■	■	■	■	■	■	■	■
PPC				■	■	■	■	■	■	■		
PPC Landing Page				■	■							
Reporting	■	■	Q1 REVIEW	■	■	Q2 REVIEW	■	■	Q3 REVIEW	■	Q4 REVIEW	
Biweekly Meetings	■	■	■	■	■	■	■	■	■	■	■	■

This graphic illustrates our high-level calendar plan that is included in our marketing strategies. It is leveraged as more of a general document of intent, as we know the details will change as time goes by.

The details of your strategy and how you wish to document implementation are up to you. The key is to make sure you have your implementation plan documented in writing or mapped out in our project management system. After all, a goal is just an idea if it is not strategically planned.

At SyncShow, we will not take on a new client without a strategy-first approach. I cannot tell you how many clients wanted to skip this step and decided to work with another agency that would, only to come back later due to lagging results. Without a formal marketing strategy defined in writing, you will be operating reactively versus proactively, and ROI will be very difficult to attain. Don't skimp on the details when building your strategy. The amount of detail and effort you put in upfront will correlate to the results you achieve in the future.

In this chapter, we laid the groundwork for your strategic marketing plan, incorporating ROI-driven goals and your ideal customer profile. We also helped you build a three-year vision for your marketing operations and explained how to incorporate inbound and outbound marketing into one comprehensive plan. Once finished with your plan, you should have crafted a twelve-month marketing calendar, highlighting key objectives and tactical initiatives. This calendar will be your true north and your compass for success.

GOLD STANDARDS

When composing your company's marketing strategy, ask yourself the following questions:

1. Do you have an inbound marketing and outbound marketing strategy integrated into one overarching strategy, including search engine optimization, social media, content marketing, and conversion strategies?
2. Do you have an ideal customer profile defined to guide your marketing strategy?
3. Have you identified your decision-maker and influencer personas, and are you leveraging that data in all marketing materials?
4. Is your marketing strategy tied to SMART (specific, measurable, attainable, realistic, and timely) goals?

If you answered yes to all four of these questions, you are well on your way to having a strong ROI-driven marketing strategy. If you answered no to any of the questions, it's time to step back and rethink your plan.

MARKETING TEAM STRUCTURE

Without a strong marketing team—the right people in the right seats—it doesn't matter how hard you work or how correctly things are done; you just won't scale and attain the type of 10X ROI you're looking for. After all, we've all heard the saying, "If you want to go far, go together."

So let's get under the hood of it. If you're looking to go far, setting up the right team is the first step to going the distance.

Marketing teams are similar to sports teams in that you need coaches, A-team starting players, developing team players, and logistics team members. In general, the ROI-driven marketing team has accountabilities that fall under four categories. You can fill any of these accountabilities with your own marketing team, contractors, or a marketing agency:

- Strategists = Coaches
- Project Managers = Logistics
- Specialists = A-Team Starting Players
- Implementers = Developing Team Players

Before we break down each of these roles and responsibilities and how they serve to grow your organization, it's important to note that your own team is largely going to be built around the size of your organization. So first, let's look at what marketing teams look like by organization size when they are built successfully for the current state but are also well positioned for future growth.

Marketing budgets should include salaries, tools, technology stack costs, travel expenses, hardware, and any of the inbound and outbound expenses.

IF YOUR MARKETING BUDGET
IS LESS THAN $150,000

Your first step to creating a strong marketing team is to invest in one person who can grow with your organization and then give them a marketing automation tool to leverage for efficiency. This person is typically your marketing strategist with generalist capabilities.

This person is a crucial hire for your business because if hired correctly, they can grow with your organization and your team to become a strong leader who has exponential growth in their own career with your company. This person will likely be more junior—not a ton of experience in the field but enough that they can grasp the needs and drive forward. This person will learn as they do. Ideally, they should be a bit more entrepreneurial and self-starting because you'll need them to be confident enough to take the marketing plan and run with it. They'll be more of a utility player because at this point, you won't be able to hire out for much else.

For the remainder of your budget, our recommendation is to get this team member ongoing training—both in digital marketing and general professional development. This ensures you're watering your garden so you can harvest it later. In addition to training, dive into our chapter on technology stack (Chapter 12), and ensure they have a best-in-class marketing automation tool. Not only will this make your team of one more efficient, but it will also ensure they're making data-driven decisions. As a bonus, most of these tools offer ongoing education and training, so you'll likely be able to kill two birds with one stone.

IF YOUR MARKETING BUDGET
IS $151,000-$500,000

Here you have a few opportunities to add to your team of one (your strategist) and start to leverage an agency team. Because the budget is still fairly restricted, you're going to get the best bang for your buck and the strongest ROI by allocating your additional spend with your agency first. That said, this should *only* be the case if you can say yes to the following statements:

- I've found an agency I like working with, and my marketing strategist feels supported by them.
- I'm seeing year-over-year growth in KPIs and pipeline revenue goals and am confident that I'm ready to diversify my marketing efforts and spend.

If the above statements are true, this is the time to level up your spend with a deeper dive into online marketing to support your pipeline revenue goals. This likely also means allocating a portion of this budget for a strong paid media campaign, but again, only if it can prove return on investment.

IF YOUR MARKETING BUDGET
IS $500,000 AND UP

At a $500,000-plus spend, it's crucial to leverage a strong in-house team as well as agencies for the capabilities you need to hit your goals. Your strategist should be seasoned and operate as a leader on your executive team. They should have visibility into the overall growth plan of the business so they can contribute appropriately through long- and short-term strategic plans.

Due to the sheer volume of work product coming out of a team of this size, hiring a project manager or junior strategist to support your main strategist will be highly important. The other internal hire that is often easiest to bring in-house due to the sensitive nature of the outsourced work via an agency is a content specialist. Getting a dedicated writer who knows your business, customers, and industry is going to set you apart from your competitors and save a ton of headaches from working with an agency to try to fill this gap.

Content, when done correctly, is expensive, and it is so subjective. The best course of action will be to hire a content specialist who can craft a strong brand voice and then support internal and external marketing efforts. This will then allow you to leverage your agency spend deeper into the specific industry verticals that are more directly tied to ROI: paid media (Google pay per click), search engine optimization (SEO), and conversion rate optimization (CRO), to name a few.

Unfortunately, a key consideration here is to really think about what you need your agency to achieve for your growth goals at this point. Often, what got you to point B won't get you to point C. This might be the time to evaluate the ROI of the relationship and their capabilities as an agency. At this level of agency spend, you need to ensure you're still seeing the growth needed to support your business. Sometimes, this means segmenting your work into more specific agency contracts rather than giving all your work to one general, full-service agency.

SMART HIRING IS SMART BUSINESS

SyncShow had a client that grew considerably quickly while working with us. At that specific time, our agency was also rapidly evolving. While we were in growth mode, we didn't have as many senior staffers as needed to best support this account. We were focused on growing our team with long-term talent that would grow into roles at the agency. Instead of staffing this client account with senior leadership to ensure they had the support considered necessary, we leveraged the account with a midlevel account strategist who was, bluntly, in over her head.

Senior leadership would support behind the scenes, coach, and guide our strategist to best serve the client, but in the end, when it came time to renew, they didn't continue working with us. They felt (rightly) that they needed someone with more seasoned experience—someone who could predict where the puck was going. Because we didn't arm the account with the day-to-day support it deserved, we lost out on hundreds of thousands of dollars in future revenue. By the time we realized it, swooping in and saving the day at the last minute was a failed attempt to right the ship. To make things worse, the midlevel account strategist also left. We put her in a position that she was not ready for. The stress and anxiety built up, and she felt responsible for the client's departure. At the end of the day, it was my fault. I felt horrible and paid the price for the mistake.

Long story short: hire for where you're going, whether that's internal or external.

ROLES EVERY TEAM NEEDS

As stated previously, every marketing team needs certain players in order to achieve the requisite success. Let's explore those roles.

Strategists

Strategists are the coaches. Strategists are the people who have a strong grasp of ROI-driven marketing and can provide strategic direction in one or multiple verticals (i.e., email marketing, social media, search engine optimization, paid advertising, content marketing, branding).

Finding talented and experienced marketers who comprehend today's shifting landscape is difficult. These people exist, but they are elusive unicorns. When you find these people, make sure you keep them. Once you have them on our team, you need to develop **strategies** and implement **systems** and **software** to see them through. There are a lot of moving parts, and it can be overwhelming.

It's crucial that these roles be separate from the CEO or other executive leader positions (with the exception of chief marketing officer at larger organizations). After all, if you're an executive who is working *in* the business, it's nearly impossible to work *on* the business. If you want to scale and scale quickly, getting a dedicated marketing strategist is crucial.

The strategist role can be in-house or contracted via an agency, consultant, or outsourced partner. At the end of the day, this role is tasked with the why and so what of all the tactics your team is working on. They need to be high level, be focused on your goals, and have the ability to forecast where the puck is going. This role shapes the vision of how your marketing aligns with your company goals and ultimately the vision of the CEO. The marketing team member responsible for strategy must "get" the difference between vanity metrics and real ROI.

Project Managers

Project managers are the logistics people who set timelines, establish budgets, and task out work to ensure proper execution of marketing efforts, including making sure it is on time and on budget.

This role can also be in-house as a full-time hire or contracted via your agency team. This person is a taskmaster who loves to hit deadlines and is responsible for implementing the tactical plan. They should work side by side with the strategist while distributing all work among your specialists and implementers (more on that below) and/or your agency and vendor partners.

You're looking for someone who is methodical, operationally savvy, hyper-organized, and nimble using different technology tools. A good project manager is the glue of your marketing team—it doesn't matter how strong your strategist is or how skilled your specialists are if there is no one making sure the trains run on time. This role is crucial to helping you scale.

It is worth noting that it can be difficult, but not impossible, to find a person who can sit in the strategist and project manager seats simultaneously. More often than not, these roles showcase very different skills, and you should hire according to the skills first. Getting the right people in the right seats will allow you to scale and will pay off in the long run—not only with efficiency but also in the culture of your organization.

Marketing Specialists

Specialists are marketing A-team starting players. They typically have an advanced degree of specialization in a chosen field. Without strong specialists, your marketing will be weak. When thinking of key specialists, consider the main tenets of digital marketing:

- Search engine optimization
- Web development
- Social media
- Email marketing
- Content writing and editing
- Graphic design
- Video production
- Paid media and advertising
- Analytics and reporting
- Conversion rate optimization

THE GREAT 8 PILLARS

When hiring a specialist, look for those who have a passion and exude excitement for their area of expertise. They should be self-learners who are constantly consuming knowledge and staying on top of industry trends. A good specialist will continuously bring new ideas to the table, craft thought leadership articles, and bring your team to another level. A specialist in any of the areas above should be able to provide examples of their work and answer detailed questions about their areas of expertise. We typically find that these specialists are not client facing, and many don't want to be. Therefore, interpersonal and presentation skills are not always needed.

Implementers

Implementers are the developing team members. They are typically generalists who implement the strategies and timelines dictated by strategists, project managers, or specialists. They are typically accountable for publishing and execution of the work developed by the specialists.

When hiring an implementer, we look for candidates who have a high level of attention to detail and a basic understanding of marketing, including social media, SEO, conversion rate optimization, and website maintenance. Implementers interact with many team members, so communication skills are very important. Since implementers are developing team members, we look for college graduates who are still feeling their way into marketing and may not know what area of marketing they want to focus their career on. They may become a specialist, project manager, or strategist, or they may fall in love with implementation. Your goal is to hire the best and help them succeed so that they can grow into their area of preference.

Although a full team of this support might look like a wish list, even for the largest of organizations, start by thinking about your specialist team as where you'll get the most bang for your buck. Do you want to invest in a full-time hire in any of these roles based on the amount of work needed to best support your go-to-market strategy? If one role seems as if it will dominate in hours compared to others and it will stay the course for some time to come, start there.

WHEN AN AGENCY CAN MAKE A DIFFERENCE

Hiring an agency is often a more cost-effective and ROI-driven way to get access to this large list of specialties. There are three distinct approaches you can take with this:

1. **Hire a full-service digital marketing agency** to support your strategy, project management, specialty, and implementation needs. This outsourced partner becomes your marketing team and will relieve you of needing to hire, manage, and train a team. This is often the easiest way to work with an agency for success. They become an extension of your team— they just happen to get paid by a different company and sit in a different office. Sometimes, you can negotiate shared office time to have your main team on-site at your company; this is usually dependent on how large your engagement is with the agency.

2. **Work with an agency on one or several specific tactics**, such as SEO, to support specific specialty needs. If you have an in-house marketing team or person, there are many instances where complementing your team with agency support shows strong returns. Not only does this allow each person and role to focus on what they've been hired for, but they can also collaborate and learn from each other for stronger outcomes.

   A benefit of hiring an agency is ensuring that you have access to the freshest knowledge in an ever-changing space. This proves especially fruitful in specialties because they are so nuanced. Often, agencies will specialize by industry or service, and if you have a partial in-house team, getting specific support in one tactic can make all the difference to proactively fill the gaps in your strategic plan.

3. **Hire only your strategist, and outsource everything else to an agency**. This is prudent for several reasons. Ensuring you have a person in your company who is accountable to steer the ship gives it the best chance of success. This person should oversee all marketing, not just digital marketing, and then leverage the agency for additional strategic support and all digital tactical support to meet their goals and needs. Aside from accountability, this is a sustainable way to grow your business through marketing without putting unrealistic expectations on your in-house marketing person.

Either way, by using an agency in a full or partial capacity, you can often achieve your goals without having to recruit, hire, train, and retain each of these team members. Agencies that have a proven track record of success invest in their people and the training that goes along with each of these specialties in an ever-changing industry that requires constant continuing education.

Think of your marketing team as a sports team. Investing in these folks, training and developing them, and giving them time to grow is what's going to take you from a minor league to a major league team. These decisions are crucial and need to be nurtured accordingly. As you grow your agency team, look for an agency that acts as a partner and not as a vendor. These people are on your team, and you want a team that's invested to win. Culturally, this will make all the difference. Remember that partnership is a two-way street, so you'll want to make sure they know they're a part of your team too!

Your marketing team is only as strong as your weakest member. Whether you opt to hire internally, hire an agency, or adopt a hybrid approach, it is your responsibility to ensure that your team is sound. Ultimately, your team should comprise strategists, project managers, specialists, and implementers. If your budget is small, you may have one or two people fulfilling all these roles. If this is the case, it is important to recognize the traits and accountabilities that make each role successful. Over the years, we have found that very few people can successfully execute in more than one role, let alone all of them simultaneously. If you are a great project manager, you are most likely wired differently than a great strategist and vice versa. Your responsibility is to honestly assess your team's players and whether they are in the best positions.

GOLD STANDARDS

When it comes time to staff your marketing team, consider the following:

1. Do you have dedicated strategists and project managers (separate from C-suite leaders)?

2. Do you have the necessary supporting marketing specialists and implementation team members to achieve your goals?

3. Do your marketing and sales teams operate as a cohesive unit with shared goals, transparency, accountability, alignment, and reporting?

4. Does your company have resources for each of the following specialty roles for your marketing specialists and implementation team (recommended in-house, agency, or contractor, depending on size of company or budget)?
   a. Conversion rate optimization
   b. Photography and video
   c. Data analysis and analytics
   d. Content writer/editor and proofreading
   e. Graphic design
   f. Search engine optimization

5. Do your specialists and implementation team meet these qualifications?
   a. Three-plus years' experience
   b. Focused on production, not on operations
   c. Follow the process and don't create their own
   d. Really strong communicators
   e. Results driven and detail oriented
   f. Empathetic approach and service-based approach

6. Does your marketing strategist meet these qualifications?

a. Responsible for captaining the ship, *not* implementation. This role may be in-house or outsourced to an agency or contractor and includes the following:
    i. Not afraid to take a leadership role even with CEOs
    ii. Mentoring, training, holding team accountable
    iii. Reporting to executive team
    iv. Finding weaknesses and shoring them up
    v. Hiring and onboarding
    vi. Analyzing metrics
    vii. Forecasting
    viii. Budgeting
b. Operations minded, not a tactician
c. Both people oriented and process oriented (balance)
d. Should understand both marketing and sales
e. Had a successful career in marketing but realized they're more of a leader

7. Does your marketing project management team or person have these qualifications?

a. Responsible for the oversight of roadmap implementation, which includes the following:
    i. Not afraid to take a leadership role even with CEOs
    ii. Project timelines and schedules
    iii. Communications
    iv. Project scope and budget tracking
    v. Assignment of tasks and monitoring
b. Process minded, detail oriented
c. Should understand project management tools and systems
d. May have worked in marketing but recognized they prefer process

If you answered yes to five or more of these questions, then you are well on your way to having an ROI-driven marketing team. If you answered no to three or more of the questions, you may want to evaluate your team to ensure you have the right people in the right seats to pull off a successful ROI-driven marketing program.

THE ALMIGHTY WEBSITE

Your digital front door. Your messaging megaphone. Your reputation presentation. Your product and service showcase. Your website is the most valuable asset in your sales and marketing ecosystem.

In Chapter 7, we guided you in developing a kick-ass value proposition. In Chapter 8, we helped you build an ROI-driven marketing strategy. This chapter is all about building an ROI-driven machine that attracts and converts customers while you sleep. What we are not going to cover is things like SEO best practices or user interface designs. This chapter is about websites that provide a return on investment and some of the things we see that most marketers miss. It's time to get serious about your website.

Your ROI-driven marketing strategy will largely focus on attracting and converting buyers into customers, essentially pulling them from where they are today (point A) and pushing them to your website (point B). The diagram illustrates the digital marketing ecosystem. Starting on the bottom left, you leverage inbound and outbound marketing tactics to create brand awareness and educate your prospects during their research stage. When done properly, these tactics should drive qualified traffic to your website, where you continue to build trust and familiarize prospects with your brand.

Your website is the heart of your ecosystem; that's why we placed it in the middle of the ecosystem. It would be great if prospective customers called and said, "I want to be your customer—let's go," but they don't. Today, buyers don't want to talk to you unless they have to. They prefer to get all their information in advance, and they want this information quickly. Only when they have completed all their research, assessed their options, and analyzed competitors are they ready to engage and take the next step by reaching out to you for more information. Your website must help them take that next step.

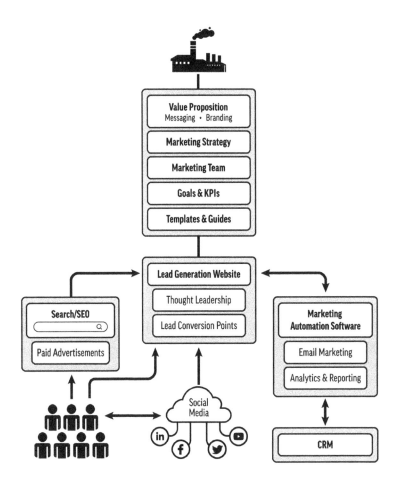

The ROI-driven website has eight main objectives:

1. Attract qualified buyers.
2. Present a professional image of your organization.

3. Educate, inform, and excite buyers about how you will help them succeed.
4. Educate and inform buyers about your company, products, and services.
5. Clearly illustrate how easy it is to do business with you.
6. Build trust with your audience.
7. Encourage and solicit your visitors to take the next step in engaging with your organization.
8. Collect information on visitors' needs and interests and deliver it to the sales and marketing teams.

These are the primary objectives in an ROI-driven website and the focus of this chapter. Think of your website as your buyer's trusted friend, an all-knowing Yoda who is there to guide them to success.

WHAT IS AN ROI-DRIVEN WEBSITE?

This is actually pretty simple. An ROI-driven website is one that converts visitors into qualified leads or can be proven to add significant value to the buyer during the buying process, leading to sales revenue. Ideally, your website's backbone, the content management system (CMS), should have a CRM integrated so that you can track leads through the sales pipeline to closed customer.

If you are not familiar with the term CRM, it stands for customer relationship management, and it is a specific type of software that enables companies to better serve their customers. Over the last twenty years, CRM has taken on a broad range of capabilities and meanings. Companies like Salesforce have built a highly customizable software platform that can be modified to meet almost any customer service need, while others like HubSpot offer out-of-the-box solutions including marketing automation, sales and pipeline management, operations capabilities, and more.

Our reference to CRM is specifically related to the sales process and sales pipeline capabilities. When your website is properly integrated with CRM software, it makes tracking ROI much easier.

How Big Should My Website Be?

For the past decade or so, content marketing experts have recommended that companies create copious amounts of content and append that content to their websites to assist in positioning themselves as thought leaders and improving search engine rankings. Some marketers have taken these recommendations to the extreme and believe that more blogs, more videos, more, more, more will help them achieve success.

The result is that website page counts have scaled out of control, and much of the content being created is worthless junk. I have seen this countless times when analyzing websites. A new client will inform me that they have thirty-five to fifty pages on their website, and we run some tests and find they have over four hundred!

There is no magic answer to how many pages you need for an ROI-driven website. Your page count should not be determined based on a specific number. Ideally, you want as many pages as necessary to meet the eight objectives above and no more. I have seen smaller websites with as few as ten pages perform exceptionally well. I have also seen websites with hundreds of pages perform equally well. It all depends on the goals for your website.

My recommendation is to analyze your sitemap and look at every page. Ask yourself, "What is the value of this page?" If it is not valuable, get rid of it, combine pages, or craft a new page strategy.

Before deleting any existing page from your website, you must assess the SEO value of that page. I have seen marketing agencies build new websites for companies without consideration of the SEO value of their existing site pages, only to launch a new site and see traffic drop 40 to 50 percent overnight. To assess a specific webpage, we recommend that you use SEMRush, Screaming Frog, or Google Analytics to inform your decision.

What about My Blog or Resource Center?

Within your website, we recommend a blog area or resource center that houses your thought leadership content. This section of your website should scale over time. Expert content that truly educates, informs, and excites your buyers is very important. More is better in this regard, as this content will help improve your search engine rankings and can also be used within your inbound and outbound marketing efforts.

However, it's important to recognize that we used the term "expert content." Don't create content just for SEO value. Your content must be valuable to your ideal buyer. If it does not educate, inform, and excite, then it's not worthy of being put on your website.

What Technologies Should My Website Employ?

This is a question that I get asked frequently. Similar to page count, there is no magic number of technologies as long as you have the tools to get the job done.

Let's start with your content management system (CMS). Your CMS is the backbone of your website and is critical in ROI-driven websites. Why? A strong CMS will be more efficient and save you time and money. If your CMS is outdated or ineffective, you will spend countless hours and dollars on maintenance and security issues. If you are looking to attain an ROI from your website, you must look at all aspects of your website. Cheaper does not necessarily mean better.

There is a plethora of great CMS platforms out there, and over the years we have used many of them. Each CMS has unique features and functionality that may be required for your specific needs. My experience with ROI-driven websites is that two CMS platforms have stood out: HubSpot and WordPress, with a preference for HubSpot. We develop on both platforms and will always be open to other options. Our objective is to choose the best one for the situation. Our experience thus far is that HubSpot is superior for ROI-driven lead machines, but you can still get the job done with just about any other platform as long as it meets the eight objectives above and the gold standards at the end of this chapter.

We recommend that you do the research and find a platform that works best for your organization. When assessing your CMS platform, consider the following:

1. **Ease of Maintenance**: Test out each CMS and perform routine maintenance tasks.
   a. Is it intuitive, or does it require training?
   b. Is the CMS easy to navigate?
   c. Does it effectively update your desktop and mobile sites equally well or require additional testing?
   d. Does the CMS offer different user access levels?

2. **Security**: Look at historical reports on the security of the CMS. The last thing you want is for pornography to be injected into your site or to have your website taken offline by a hacker (yes, we have seen both).
   a. How often must it be updated, and can you effectively handle routine security updates?
   b. Does the CMS require third-party plug-ins to achieve the functionality you desire? If so, are the plug-ins secure and supported?

3. **Hosting Features and Costs**: Some CMS platforms, such as HubSpot, provide the CMS as a software in a service package with hosting included. Other

CMS platforms, such as WordPress, require you to find your own hosting.

    a. Do you prefer multiple vendors or a single vendor?

    b. Will these hosting companies provide routine security updates and feature/function enhancements, or will you have to do this?

    c. Does your hosting provider offer a content delivery network (CDN)?

    d. Will the hosting provider ensure your security certificate (SSL) is updated?

    e. Does the hosting provider have multiple backups and redundancy?

    f. Where are the hosting provider's servers located?

    g. What are the monthly hosting costs and total cost of ownership?

4. **Support**: Some CMS platforms offer amazing support while others little. Review your options and choose wisely.

    a. When you need support for your CMS, will it be available?

b. Is there adequate online support available? This may be in the form of a help desk, documentation, videos, or call center.

5. **Templates and Integrations**:
   a. Does the CMS platform have a bevy of user interface design templates to choose from?
   b. Does it support third-party integrations easily, or will it require a custom application programming interface (API) to be developed?

When building an ROI-driven website, it's important to look at all these factors, as each one can significantly impact your total cost of ownership, affecting your return on investment.

Beyond your CMS, there are other integrated software and technologies that we recommend for ROI-driven marketing. We will cover more on these technologies in Chapter 12.

How Do I Integrate My Value Proposition?

Integrating your value proposition effectively is so important. We suggest that you look at Donald Miller's book *Building a StoryBrand* (*StoryBrand.com*). His methodology will provide you with a very effective template for your value proposition messaging that buyers will relate to. Until you have a chance to read his book or take his certification course, you have a couple of options. You can work with a writer to ensure your value proposition elements are worked into your website's editorial copy, or you can hire a certified StoryBrand guide.

Once you have your value proposition messaging laid out, you need to integrate it throughout your website. Ideally, you don't want to reiterate the same sentences; however, you want to ensure the story you are trying to convey is supported on every page. Visitors may enter your website from any page, not necessarily the home page, so you will need to look at each page and determine which elements of your story are applicable. Provided below are some examples:

- **Home Page**: Traditionally, we recommend that your home page completely spell out your entire value proposition with language that communicates the following:
    - How your organization is uniquely positioned.
    - How you understand your buyer's pain points and challenges.

- How your organization is uniquely qualified to solve those pain points and challenges.
- What steps the buyer needs to take to engage and start to do business with you.

- **About Us**: The About Us page should support your value proposition messaging. This is another chapter in your story. How does your company structure, history, core values, and so on support your unique stance in the marketplace? What is it about your company that supports your unique positioning?

- **Product and Service Pages**: These pages should support the value proposition as well. How are your products or services designed to uniquely satisfy your buyer's pain points and challenges? Features and functions or processes may be a piece of this puzzle. However, you should focus not on what these features, functions, and processes are but on how they benefit your buyer and help them achieve success.

- **Supporting Collateral**: Every asset you have on your website (e.g., case studies, testimonials,

THE GREAT 8 PILLARS

white papers, videos, downloads) should support your value proposition claims. Having a customer testimonial about how fast your delivery was is nice, but if your value proposition does not stand on your speed to market, then this testimonial is a part of your story that just confuses buyers. Not all positive, well-written, or well-designed content is appropriate. Review all your marketing and sales assets, and ask yourself, "Does this support the value proposition claims?" If not, rework it or remove it.

An easy way to see whether your website is geared toward your buyer is to read the editorial copy and digest the supporting materials. If these materials state, "We are the best because..." or "We do this," and "We do that," then your website is probably all about you, and buyers will reject the message. Make your website all about your buyer, and help them achieve success.

Website Page-Level Strategy

Visitors may enter your website from any page, not necessarily the home page, so you will need to look at each page and craft a page-level strategy. Each page should have a purpose. Some common purposes include:

- To educate, inform, or excite
- To solicit buyer engagement
- To collect information about the buyer
- To instill trust
- All of the above

Some pages will have more than one purpose. We recommend that you review each page of your website to see. whether it meets any of the purposes above. If not, delete it or rework it.

Ask yourself:

- Is this page necessary?
- Does it support our value proposition?
- Does it build trust?
- Does it have the proper calls to action to solicit buyer engagement?
- Does it have the proper imagery and supporting content to educate, inform, or excite the buyer?
- Is there an opportunity to collect buyer information effectively?
- How does this page assist the buyer in progressing through the buying process?

LEAD MACHINE

A couple of years ago, we began working with a small manufacturer of safety products. They were looking to scale and needed some help with marketing. After we completed the Diagnostic and Roadmap and built out their marketing strategy, we determined that they were essentially starting from scratch when it came to marketing. They required a significant focus on infrastructure and a new website. Unfortunately, the client's budget did not support a new website build in addition to the other marketing and sales priorities they so desperately needed. The website was put on hold.

As we began our engagement, it was agreed that the marketing strategy was to focus on infrastructure, not ROI. However, we were instructed to begin lead generation once the infrastructure was ready to support such activities. Several months later, we began reporting on lead flow, the agreed-upon goals, and key performance indicators. Website traffic was increasing, and engagement rates were up, but leads were flat.

We reiterated the need for a new website. Eventually the client agreed, and we built a new website for them.

Within a couple of months after launching the website, the lead flow increased significantly. Within six months of launch, leads had increased by over 230 percent!

Don't underestimate the power of a strong website.

Your website is often the first point of contact a buyer has with your business. It also takes a significant investment in time and money to craft a website that will drive more closed sales. Whether you are a small business with a website budget of $35,000 or a larger business with a budget of more than $250,000, you deserve a website that performs.

If you have not taken a really good look at your website lately, now is the time. Many manufacturers dismiss the value of a strong website, and this is a big mistake. Countless times we have seen our clients earn million-dollar and multimillion-dollar contracts through a newly built website. Trust me when I say that today's buyers are looking at your website. They are also looking at your competitors' websites. The sites that instill trust, communicate value, and present a professional image get more business. Period.

In this chapter, we discussed the key elements of an ROI-driven website. If your website is not performing well and not delivering results, the answer to your problem lies somewhere in this chapter. It is also important to remember that your website is not a one-time project that you build, launch, and forget. It's a living, breathing asset that should be refined continually.

GOLD STANDARDS

To assist you in ensuring that your website meets the standards for an ROI-driven program, use the following questions to assess your website or new build:

1. Is your website clear, simple, and easy to navigate?
2. Does your website leverage video?
3. Does your organization have clear and strong calls to action on its site?
4. Does your website have clear pathways for engagement?
5. Does your website have a clear process for how prospects can do business with you?
6. Is your website built on a strong content management system?

7. Is your website mobile-friendly?
8. Is Google Analytics connected to your website?
9. Do your website analytics meet industry standards?
10. Is your website free of spelling and grammar mistakes?
11. Is your website free of broken links or missing pages?
12. Has your organization performed SEO keyword research and incorporated it into site content?
13. Are your SEO rankings monitored via SEO software?
14. Does your site have unique H1s, title tags, and meta descriptions?
15. Are your website's redirects set up properly?
16. Does your website have a solid backlink profile?
17. Are all site images optimized for SEO?
18. Is Google Search Console connected to your site?
19. Have you generated and submitted your sitemap?
20. Does your site have an SSL certificate?
21. Do you have a robots.txt file created?
22. Does your website page speed meet or exceed industry standards?
23. Does your website have proper schema markup?
24. Is Google Tag Manager set up?
25. Does your organization's site have an SEO-friendly URL structure?

26. Does your website meet accessibility standards and regulations?
27. Do you have a chatbot or live chat on your site?
28. Does your website have ample content to support SEO goals?
29. Does your website have a dedicated phone number in the header for visitors to call?

If you answered no to any of these questions, we suggest that you add them to your to-do list. All of them are important to your ROI-driven strategy.

ANALYTICS AND REPORTING

"Garbage in, garbage out." "What gets measured gets managed." Pick your platitude about measurement—there certainly are a lot to choose from, but in many clichés there lies a kernel of truth. This is no different when it comes to measuring your success in online marketing.

We as marketers spend hours upon hours of effort crafting strategies and discussing the nuances of audience development, channel messaging, value propositions, and the myriad other elements that go into crafting a holistic strategy that drives people to action. But what good is theory, and even practice, if you can't accurately measure results? We end up being Sisyphean in our efforts, consistently pushing the proverbial marketing rock uphill over and over again with no real, concrete, and measurable progress. What good is effort if you don't have outcomes, and you can't know outcomes without accurate measurement.

Once your marketing strategy is in place, you need to be looking at accurate information to make data-based decisions to enhance or modify your actions. Actionable insights are one of the main differentiators against traditional advertising. If we're not utilizing this feature, we may as well buy a billboard on the side of a highway. Online marketing is surgical, omnipresent, and, above all else, innumerably measurable.

Look at your own marketing: do you have tracking set on appropriate channels where your data is being collected? If so, don't pat yourself on the back just yet. There's only one thing worse than collecting no data, and it's collecting inaccurate data. If you have no data points from which to reference, you're blind, but if you're referencing bad data, you're dangerous.

Many agency owners have worked with clients who have prided themselves on data collection, touting their ability to track year-over-year data points and reward or reprimand staff based on outcomes, but as data enthusiasts are apt to say, there are three kinds of lies in the world: lies, damn lies, and statistics. A shrewd marketer can make data speak any language with any outcome they like. An ignorant marketer can actually do the same, viewing their outcomes through whichever lens they choose since they have no frame of reference.

LESSON LEARNED

BEWARE OF ASSUMPTIONS

We've worked with large, multibillion-dollar companies whose footprints straddled oceans but whose data was so corrupted by bad tracking they were potentially hemorrhaging thousands of dollars in marketing investments without accurately tracking ROI. Take, for instance, a company that saw a nearly overnight doubling in their organic traffic reporting (nonpaid website visits derived from searches on search engine platforms like Google and Yahoo.). Their marketing staff should have known better. Organic visitation is generally not something that doubles overnight. Search engine optimization, the science of improving organic-based visitation to your websites, is something that generally takes substantial time to improve with high-yield, longtime results to site visitation, interaction, and ultimately conversion.

Coming onto the account, our data analyst looked at these items as anomalies to be questioned, not victories to be celebrated—at least not initially. Although an agency never wants to squelch a client's enthusiasm, we'd be an ineffective partner if we became yes-men and toadies; we'd only help you lose money faster.

The data being pulled in by this organization was indeed impressive, a 100 percent growth in traffic seemingly overnight. When asked what they thought prompted this increase, they responded with assured words like "this and that," with conjecture stated as fact.

Knowing the truth about your data is among the first steps in utilizing it. To us, an anomaly needs confirmation before celebration. As such, we looked at a few common reasons behind this type of immediate doubling. It is in the nature of marketers to be doubters, thinkers, and detectives; a good marketer starts with their gut, researches through detective work, and verifies through science.

The first place we often look is to see whether the data collection tool itself is functioning or set up well.

After all, machines don't yet have independent thought, and data collection and aggregation tools will grab raw data, but it's humans who provide context and initiate parameters, with installation of the tool being one of those key parameters. It turns out that one of the factors this client touted as the reason for their organic user increase was all the technical updates they were making to their site—and this could have been a factor, as technical enhancements, especially around site speed, have a significant impact on organic keyword rankings and thus search and site visits. When we asked what elements they updated, we discovered these were more closely aligned to user experience and interaction with the site, the addition of new functionality and imagery, and other areas—none of which were directed at site speed enhancements but rather the opposite. Many people added code and content that would bloat site loads and decrease organic rank.

"But Google likes updated websites, so we're being rewarded for it," they said. This can be true, but again, that was an assumption based on their desire to see information how they wanted to see it, not how it actually was. Bias overwrites data; it's a human condition. If Google or any other search algorithm were rewarding them for their efforts, then the results would still be gradual, not overnight, so even if this were true, it begs a timing issue. Search engine crawlers take time to recrawl, reindex, and rerank a site based on updates; this can take weeks for a large site and months for a smaller one, but never overnight—something else was going on.

So we dug in. We started with an assumption that the tool was misconfigured. If we started with the data itself, we'd be working in the wrong direction. If your key won't open your car, you don't start by taking the lock apart and inspecting the mechanism; you look at the key. Do you even have the right key in your hand? In this case, we checked to see that they were look-ing at the right analytics account. What we found was good news/bad news. They had the right key and were looking at their site's data; that was the good news. The bad news was that they had two of the exact same keys on their site. Through one of their updates, they installed the same analytics code twice on their site.

What's the big deal, right? Well, software will do exactly what it's told and nothing else. So what's the goal of analytics software? It's to collect data, and that's exactly what it was doing. That's exactly what both of them were doing. Two codes were firing and collecting the same data, twice, every time, on every page, for every visit. Needless to say, we found the reason for their doubling of data.

Unfortunately, because the data had been sitting that way for a while, they were going to feel the effects of this mistake for years to come. They now sat with inaccurate data that they could not parse out, other than by dividing by half, but that makes tracking a chore and inaccurate in some data points without additional math. Creating comparative data sets that included this chunk of time now came with an asterisk every time they were going to pull data.

They'd eventually outgrow the anomaly, but it would be a reminder of their poor data management for some time to come, and who knows how many macro or micro decisions were made off of bad data before it was caught. Let's just hope money wasn't spent on bad inputs; we already know time was wasted because of it. Once it was discovered, strategies needed to be reviewed, assumptions needed to be reevaluated, and testing policies had to be adjusted to stave off any similar future issues.

So what should a company know when tracking business information tied to marketing efforts, beyond just ensuring that they trust their tools and the information they're providing? As with anything, tie efforts and reporting back to business goals. Too many people get caught in the vanity metrics or general, generic data points that are fun to look at (who doesn't like a green arrow going up?) but add no real value to their company's business goals. Why do marketing if it lives in a vacuum and runs by its own set of rules and data points? No, your marketing should be seen as a means to the ends of your business. Remember that you're doing it for a reason, and that reason is your business, not your marketing as a stand-alone. Every business's data points will be different, but generally, there are relevant metrics you want to look at, along with those we consider red herring territory for many of the manufacturing businesses we work with.

Ideally, every business should have clean metrics that allow for time-over-time comparisons. In a perfect world that extends to year over year. Why year over year? Many organizations experience fluctuations in seasonality and buying cycles aligned to their industry or client needs. If you sell commodity products, we can see an influx of data as budget cycles end and extra budget money needs to be spent before the end of the year; we also see capital equipment purchases happening to beat tax season. After all, you wouldn't expect a ski resort to post the same numbers in the summer as they do in the winter, so having a full look at the calendar year for comparison metrics makes true comparisons of growth or loss more accurate.

It's not uncommon for businesses to say they don't suffer from timing-based impacts, and sometimes when looking at the data we agree, but just as often we do see market changes in owned media analytics at predictable intervals over a set period of time. Knowing this will help you better understand your data: a month-over-month dip may still mean an increase overall if you've entered your slow time and still beat commensurate data from the year before. If you're in the scenario where you don't trust your data or maybe weren't even collecting your data, that's okay, but you have to start now.

A general goes into battle knowing the lay of the land and the history of success or failure on previous campaigns. You can still make decisions and validate them against near-term data, but just realize that you may be missing attributions. If you're worried about starting to use your data but feel defeated even before beginning, remember the adage that the best time to plant a tree was twenty years ago, and the second best time is today. So get your tracking installed. Check its veracity, and set benchmarks. Then keep revisiting the data to see whether it's all running without issue.

CHOOSING YOUR TOOLS

If you're looking to install new tracking software or are unsure which analytics platform you should use, consider this: in my experience, nine out of ten companies run their analytics through the same free tool, Google Analytics (GA). It's a powerful-enough tool that gives the majority of sites access to the information they need to make the right business decisions. There are several newer data visualization tools available now that allow further parsing of data, including Domo and Tableau, among myriad others; just remember that many of these tools don't actively collect the data but parse and display it in a way that allows for deeper analysis. If you're running Google Analytics on your site (at least at the time of this writing), then the majority of you are likely on the right track.

One nice adjustment we like that helps with GA installation is installing its firing through a container tag within Google Tag Manager (GTM). Tag management tools like GTM allow agencies or other organizations to access the website and insert code without ever logging into the site and having to manipulate core website code functionality. Think of it as a window into a website through which code can be inserted and information can be pulled out.

Why should a marketer care about this? Although it has its potential downsides, if you're in-house, it allows you to provide access to tracking code and other code insertions to a vendor without ever giving them your website log-in credentials, and it allows trusted third-party entities the ability to effect change without having to learn back-end website structure or manage multiple log-ins across multiple clients.

The biggest benefit, however, is the control it immediately gives you to allow for more surgical and repeatable tracking. For example, we can now target pixel firing or code insertion on specific pages based on user actions and dynamically generated elements, impacting hundreds of pages (or even thousands) at once with a single setup. Why does this matter? Well, when you graduate beyond tracking sessions, users, and bounce rate, you may want to parse data based on user behavior and collect data on on-page actions instead of just relevant visits. Imagine the impact of tracking data only on those people who took specific actions on your site and drawing assigned attributions and desired action. It's the equivalent of getting information on the number of people who walked through the turnstiles at a baseball stadium versus getting information on how many people bought tickets within twenty-four hours before the game, arrived, bought a beer, sat in their seat for at least seven innings, and walked through the gift shop while spending at least $50. With triggers and filtering, often utilized via these container tag tools, a sophisticated marketer can set data collection based on prerequisites. I imagine within your business there are users or actions you'd specifically like to track to help build a fuller picture to support a more nuanced strategy to support business goals and growth.

ROI-DRIVEN METRICS VERSUS MARKETING METRICS

ROI-driven marketing requires marketers to track marketing effort to sales revenue, period. The goal is to ensure the investment in marketing is providing a return. To ensure you are providing a return, you must follow your primary marketing initiatives from the first point of contact with a prospect to closed sales. Below are some of the primary metrics we define and track for our clients that assist in measuring ROI.

Define:

1. Average initial order value
2. First-year average client value
3. Customer lifetime value
4. Lead vs. marketing-qualified lead vs. sales-qualified lead
5. Lead values ($$, lead vs. marketing-qualified lead vs. sales-qualified lead)

Track:

1. Leads generated from marketing and the corresponding value ($$)
2. Marketing-qualified leads generated from marketing and the corresponding value ($$)
3. Sales-qualified leads generated from marketing and the corresponding value ($$)
4. Closed new business from marketing-generated leads and the revenue generated by these sales as illustrated in initial order value, first-year average client value, and customer lifetime value

The above metrics are what your leadership team cares about. These are the metrics your marketing reports should definitely include. Additionally, you should be tracking marketing metrics to guide your progress. Key metrics to track include:

- Sessions (number of visits to your website)
- Users (individuals who visit your site)
- New users (users who hadn't visited your site)
- Bounce rate (percent of visitors to your site who view one page, take no action, and leave)
- Average time on site (length of time, on average, users are active on your website)
- Conversions (how many users take a defined and desired action on your website, including filling out a form, purchasing a product, or clicking an on-site element)
- Channel source (where visitors came into your site, usually broken down into organic, paid, social, direct, email, and other or undefined)
- Average pages per visit (average number of pages a user views per session)

If, at a minimum, you're tracking those metrics, you'll have enough to track progress and build strategies. You may not be able to directly tie specific efforts to results down to the nth degree with these metrics, but they'll tell you which direction your efforts are pointing.

All data can be used to add insights into your marketing efforts. The seven metrics above are perhaps the most common metrics that marketers track. These metrics help to inform your successes or opportunities within specific marketing tactics. Even though they are not ROI-driven metrics, they are very important to track, measure, and respond to.

VANITY METRICS

Often, we see that marketers are tracking what we call vanity metrics. These are metrics such as likes, comments, and followers. Although these metrics can help guide your marketing efforts, they typically do not inform ROI-driven marketing. Take, for instance, likes, comments, and followers: These metrics illustrate a form of engagement with your brand; however, they don't necessarily indicate how the marketing initiative is generating an ROI. Someone may like your content or post, but that person may not be a client or prospect. Additionally, a comment or a follower does not necessarily indicate you are attracting more of your desired buyers to your brand. We are not suggesting that you abandon tracking these vanity metrics, as they can be valuable, but we just want to ensure you recognize their place in your program.

Reporting and Cadence

Data acquisition is just one piece of the puzzle. Now that you have a defined list of what to track and analyze, you need to develop standard reporting procedures. We recommend that you have standardized reporting that is distributed to your leadership team and marketing teams. Your reports should follow these guidelines:

- Be distributed monthly (at a minimum)
- Include actual data with comparisons from previous periods
- Compare actual data to your goals as outlined in Chapter 6
- Include a summary assessment of your analysis stating what actions you are taking based on the data
- Include visual representations of what data sets met, exceeded, or missed the goal illustrated by highlighted color

In addition to your monthly reporting, we recommend that you have quarterly business reviews with your leadership team with more detailed reporting and ROI metrics to ensure all parties are on the same page.

> *What gets measured gets improved.*
> **—PETER DRUCKER**

Acquiring the right data to make educated and informed decisions is critical to any ROI-driven marketing strategy. Fortunately, good, clean data is easily acquired once you know what to look for and where to look.

In this chapter, we outlined the difference between ROI-driven metrics and vanity metrics. We also provided recommendations on specifically what to track and the cadence of your reporting.

Finding and aggregating this data is also very easy once you have the right tools and standard operating procedures set up. In its most basic form, we attain all the data listed above from three main sources: Google Analytics, Google Search Console, customer relationship management, and marketing automation software. You may find additional data sources can bring even more value to your marketing program, specific to specialty tactics like social media or search engine optimization. Due to the ever-changing landscape of specialty marketing software, we decided not to provide a list of our chosen tools. We recommend you find the tools that work best for your specific strategies and invest in getting every bit of data you can to inform your marketing.

GOLD STANDARDS

When evaluating the health and relevance of your marketing team's analytics and reporting, begin with the following questions:

1. Is your Google Analytics properly set up to track relevant data and omit "bad" data?
2. Do you have Google Tag Manager set up?
3. Is Google Analytics goal tracking set up and properly firing?
4. Is your search console properly set up, error free, and tied into Google Analytics?
5. Is there a filter view in GA with a raw data view also pulling in data?

6. Is site search tracking turned on if your site has on-site search capabilities?

7. Is the time set to the time zone of your organization?

8. Is your default website URL set to the proper domain and the secure version?

9. If using Google Ads, is Google Ads connected in GA, assuming a Google Ads account exists?

10. In GA, is demographic tracking data turned on?

11. Do you have standardized reports that include ROI-driven metrics?

12. Are you sending leadership marketing reports on a monthly basis?

13. Do you have quarterly marketing business reviews with your leadership team?

14. Are you tracking the appropriate marketing metrics to inform future decision-making?

If you answered yes to at least ten of these questions, congratulations! You are well on your way to implementing best practices in your marketing data analytics and reporting infrastructure. For any questions you answered no to, we recommend you work toward these adjustments for enhanced effectiveness.

TECHNOLOGY STACK

Digital tools and software usually fall into one of two categories: life changing or a total and complete waste of money. More often than not, it's not the tool but the training and onboarding of the tool that makes or breaks its usability.

We can all think of tools that make our lives better and easier at work or at home. Google color-coded calendars, Evernote to-do lists, and Slack and Zoom for remote work success are all crucial for the day-to-day of many marketers. That said, there are several tool types we couldn't live without when it comes to ROI-driven marketing—our methods and successes are built upon strong tool use. These include but aren't limited to marketing automation, customer relationship management, SEM software, data aggregators for reporting, call-tracking software, and heat mapping. When integrated, these tools give us the closed-loop reporting and data we need to make the best decisions for a 10X marketing ROI.

The right technology can help make you more efficient and effective, so don't let this area of your business become an afterthought. By building the right tech stack, you can expect value in tangible ways, such as:

- **Utilized Efficiency**: Your team can work more effectively, spending time on the areas of the business that are most impactful. Not only will this mean your team is more profitable, but they'll also be able to accomplish more in less time.

- **Streamlined Deliverables**: Less gets missed thanks to automation and reminders to keep work products flowing.

- **Better and Faster Decisions**: Utilizing tools will make your data organized and readable in a simple way, allowing team members to make better and faster decisions.

- **Team Retention**: Tools that allow team members to row in the same direction eliminate unnecessary stress and encourage longevity, not only reducing recruiting and replacement fees but also eliminating lost knowledge.

To reiterate, here are the basic tech necessities for ROI-driven marketing:

- Marketing automation such as HubSpot, Salesforce Marketing Cloud, and Pardot
- A CRM (customer relationship management) tool such as Salesforce, HubSpot, or Microsoft Dynamics

It's crucial that your organization owns these, and this is where we'll dig in the deepest. Other tools of consideration include:

- Data aggregators/reporting tools such as Databox
- SEO tools such as SEMRush or Screaming Frog
- Website heat mapping to understand usability, such as Hot Jar

IT TAKES MORE THAN TOOLS

Prior to working with us, one of our clients had been through three different CRM tools: Zoho, Salesforce, and a homegrown tool they built to better fit their business needs. None of these were successful for our client. They said, "CRM doesn't work for us—we're sick of investing time and money into tools that don't make a difference in our business."

We hear this all the time, and it is usually not the tool.

In reality, our client wasn't willing or able to onboard any of these tools successfully. While they may have signed the contract on the dotted line, they weren't ready to commit to the cultural shift it would require of their team members. They weren't willing to invest the discipline to find success.

Are there bad tools? Sure, but more often than not, we need to look in the mirror and accept some responsibility when these things don't work out.

To set your business up for success, we'll dive into the use case and recommendations around each of the crucial tools. Below are the tools, features, and considerations that meet our expectations of use to help businesses scale their sales and marketing efforts through one cohesive revenue team.

MARKETING AUTOMATION

Welcome back to working smarter, not harder. Technology is a gift, and marketing automation (MA) is akin to the invention of fire if you're in the marketing world. The right marketing automation tool gives you data you need to work smarter, freeing up time for the things you need and want to do to really drive business results.

At SyncShow, we're platinum partners of the business software HubSpot. HubSpot began as a marketing automation tool and now covers the spectrum of business automation for growing companies. We use their marketing automation and CRM for ourselves and many of our clients. While we love HubSpot, there are many tools and options to choose from.

There are a number of considerations for a successful marketing automation tool. First and foremost, are all marketing team members working out of a single best-in-class marketing automation tool like HubSpot, SharpSpring, Marketo, or Pardot? If not, it is crucial you create a business case to support the best tool for your needs. Again, we use HubSpot for our needs.

To make better marketing decisions from your tactical work, most of the action points on your website should flow through your marketing automation—not only for use of updates but also for data-tracking abilities so you can see what's working and what's not to better streamline your work. For example, calls to action need to be coded for data tracking and built in your MA. This way you can see what pages/campaigns are driving the most clicks for conversions. With this insight, you know which pages of your site drive the most important business actions, showing you the data you need to support more investment in those pages.

Other examples of this are as follows:

Workflows

Workflows are a tool that can help level up your marketing and remove the active thought process required to be everywhere all the time. Workflows are the automation in marketing automation that, when deployed effectively, make all the difference in how you do business internally as well as how you market, or nurture, externally.

Ensure internal workflows are utilized for form notifications and follow-up. This is part of what you're buying in the tool, so turn these on ASAP.

What's an internal workflow? We're glad you asked, especially since they're so helpful to business. An internal workflow is any "if this, then that" sequence of events that then deploys an internal email to your team members. This information is for internal company use only. A few examples:

- When someone downloads a specific piece of content from your website, a team member can get an email alerting them to that download. This is an applicable situation for form submissions as well.

- When someone visits your website or opens an email, you can trigger an internal email to alert a specific salesperson or multiple people of that activity to streamline follow-up when it matters most.

Ensure external automated workflows are set up and deployed on an appropriate delay to reengage online leads. This is a simple nurture campaign that can be deployed based on past actions from your leads.

External workflows are outward-facing emails; these should be branded with your company voice and are marketing email collateral content pieces. These touchpoints often "feel" like 1:1 emails but are pre-drafted and set with personalization tokens based on activities the recipient previously completed.

Metrics

Tying back to your goals, your MA needs to be specifically designed for executing, tracking, and reporting on marketing activity. This will showcase the leading key performance indicators that are making the biggest impact toward your goals.

Marketing leads should be tracked from the original point of contact through closed won or closed lost—again, allowing you to understand what marketing aspects are the biggest drivers of your closed customers.

Ensure marketing leads are categorized by life cycle; not only does this help keep your database clean, but it also allows for more in-depth segmentation for your marketing efforts, allowing marketing and sales to provide the right solution-oriented messaging at the right time when it matters most.

Communication for One Revenue Team

Keeping and utilizing a clean database will be your ultimate favor to your future self and your future revenue team. Therefore, ensure all marketing touchpoints are recorded at the contact and company records.

Select an MA tool that supports automation of rote process-related tasks. Not only is this great for your marketing team, but it is crucial for sales team members who are juggling multiple deals and deal stages that all require personal attention.

For truly seamless communication, your MA tool and your CRM need to be connected and set up to share relevant sales and marketing data and pipeline information. When looking for an integration (if you're not moving forward with an all-in-one solution like HubSpot), make sure your CRM integration provides the following:

- Automated communications or follow-up sequences
- Sales team alignment
- Lead flows and pipeline measurement
- Data and knowledge flow from marketing to sales
- Consistent and accurate account- and contact-level data, including intelligence and insights on contact behavior

- Lead tracking from first point of contact through their buying journey to sales close

These integrations are what needs to pass into your marketing automation and then pass back through the CRM. It's what's called a two-way integration, and this is crucial to a constantly changing pipeline for clear marketing and sales communication.

CUSTOMER RELATIONSHIP MANAGEMENT (CRM)

For the purpose of this book, we recommend you look at your CRM in simple terms:

1. Do you have a CRM in place? If not, get one.
2. Does it tie in to your marketing?

Optimizing your CRM for your company's sales process and sales team is an entirely different chapter in a different book, and as a salesperson myself, I can say it's well worth the investment.

As we look at your CRM as a tool to help the marketing team understand closed revenue from their efforts and to support salespeople in nurturing closed lost deals, we need to see three important things in your CRM's structure:

- Your sales pipeline measures deal value to determine ROI from marketing-driven leads.
- You have a formal process for tracking leads and your sales pipeline.
- You have a dedicated customer pipeline for upsells and cross-sells, allowing you to grow your pipeline revenue from the people who already work with you and therefore know and like you—something that should lend itself to a shorter sales cycle!

These are the three crucial elements to showcase ROI and to understand where leads break down in the sales funnel so they can be remarketed, if appropriate.

When company revenue goals aren't being met, the first round of finger-pointing quickly begins. Marketing claims that sales isn't closing leads, and sales claims that the leads aren't valuable or that marketing isn't bringing in enough leads to make a difference to the business. Tying your marketing automation to your sales CRM takes the guesswork out of the "she said, he said" game. You don't have to pick a side; you can simply look at the data to truly understand where the breakdown is coming from. Then, instead of refereeing internal battles of politics and breaking down culture, you can actively work to solve the issue (or issues) at hand for a more productive tomorrow.

Having marketing leads flow into your sales pipeline gives full visibility into where leads are coming from and how marketing supports sales efforts, bringing sales and marketing together to collectively own the big goal of company revenue. The technology stack aligning in your favor is just one more crucial tool in your toolbox for true scalable and repeatable growth.

SHARED TOOLS, SHARED COSTS: BUDGETING FOR YOUR TECHNOLOGY STACK

While there are many benefits to onboarding the right tech stack for your organization, it's not without a financial commitment. A small to medium business should expect to spend several thousand dollars a year to maintain their technology stack. For reference, a marketing budget for a manufacturing company typically ranges from 6 to 8 percent of total revenue. A portion of that budget will be allocated to your technology stack. Many tools force you to pay by seat or user (CRM) and by total database size

(MA), so these are additional considerations around cost. The larger your company, the more people who need to use the tool or be marketed to, so the more you will pay.

That said, because these tools are cross-functional and cross-departmental, it's worth investigating a shared cost for these services. Human resources, operations, and customer service all benefit from the use of a marketing automation platform and a CRM. For this reason, you should make the business case to share these costs.

In the end, if you're just getting started with building a purposeful technology stack for your company, start small. Not only will this mean you're onboarding the tools that mean the most (marketing automation and CRM), but by not biting off more than you can chew, you can ensure you're giving yourself and your team the bandwidth to onboard appropriately to ensure success in these tools for the future.

GOLD STANDARDS

Having a well-tuned tech stack can have a noticeable effect on the functionality of your marketing department. When evaluating your present or future tech stack, consider the following:

1. Do you have a formal process for tracking leads and your sales pipeline and the technology to support it?
2. Does your sales pipeline measure deal value to determine ROI from marketing-driven leads?
3. Do all marketing team members work out of a single best-in-class marketing automation tool like HubSpot, SharpSpring, Marketo, or Pardot?
4. Are your marketing automation tool and your CRM connected and set up to share relevant sales and marketing data and pipeline information?
5. Are calls to action coded for data tracking/built in your marketing automation platform?
6. Do you have internal workflows that are utilized for form notifications and follow-up?
7. Do you have automated workflows that are set up and deploying on an appropriate delay to reengage online leads?
8. Can marketing leads be tracked from the original point of contact through closed won or closed lost?
9. Are your marketing leads categorized by life cycle in your CRM?

If you answered yes to at least six of these questions, congratulations! You are well on your way to running a well-oiled technology stack that will power your marketing operations. If you answered no to more than three questions, you may need to dig in and build out a stronger tech stack to support your ROI-driven goals.

TEMPLATES AND GUIDES

I t's no surprise that hard work and determination are the cornerstone of success in a lot of life, including business. But if you want a happy life, you can't run at full speed for your entire life, or for the entire life of a company—you'll burn out. Not only that, but you'll lose money. If for every endeavor you take you have to consistently rebuild your efforts, you'll quickly hit a wall. That wall may not be energy—we all know people who never seem to run out of it—but you'll hit a wall on scalability and quality.

If you're in marketing, what you often truly need is time. You may produce a product and lend your intellectual ability and experience to complete it. It's the time and knowledge you provide that allow you to implement your marketing strategies. No matter how knowledgeable or talented you are, it is still going to take a finite amount of time to create any deliverable, and you only have so many hours you can really work to be productive. If you have inefficiencies in producing output, you're capped on the amount you can deliver.

One of the best ways to scale your and your team's availability is through templated, repeatable efforts. Now let's get something out of the way right now: a template does not mean low quality, which some folks seem to negatively equate. A template is a documented process and framework that allows you to provide a repeatable result with less effort. That old cliché that "you don't need to reinvent the wheel" does hold water.

Too often, many of us are so wrapped up in the doing of the work that we don't take the time to just write it down! It's ingrained in us and becomes somewhat like muscle memory to produce an offering. It's almost like driving home after a long day at work: one minute you're getting in your car at the office, and the next you're pulling into your driveway. You barely remember what you did in between, but you sure as heck got home the most efficient way and without thinking about it. But what happens when you want to scale? You can't drive home twice, just as you can't repeat the same hour if you're taking that hour to complete a task. You also can't outsource or bring on another producer if you haven't documented that task. After all, you can't have a random person drive from the office to your house without a map. And you can't scale your work if you don't templatize what you do to allow for growth and expansion beyond yourself.

Templates allow you to scale—you will have more hours in which to do the work by allowing others to follow your roadmap. If you've ever heard yourself or anyone else say something like, "It would take me longer to explain it than to do it," then you've likely found a need for a templated process or deliverable. It's those moments when you've siloed a specific and likely repeatable effort into one entity. This blocks scalability, even in a single deliverable, and makes you vulnerable should that knowledge walk out the door. Even if it feels as though that moment to train or document will take longer, which it likely will, consider how much future time you will save and how many hours you will open for selling and producing should that task become a templated and repeatable outcome.

In addition to templates allowing a business or an individual to scale their efforts, there's another large and measurable return on efforts with template use: quality. In our world, we work with a lot of website developers who can produce any myriad of fully baked websites on a variety of platforms. Years ago, when first starting a website, we would begin with tasking our designer with a website design, from which we'd develop website pages from a specific code set; in our world, it was usually within the HubSpot environment. We produced beautiful sites that had bespoke code that was built basically from scratch.

We did this because we thought that was how you created unique websites that performed for our clients—and they did. But these sites were expensive, time-consuming, and apt to require frequent bug fixes due to custom code; additionally, since we would use custom code for development, we often ran into version compatibility issues with certain website functionality. For example, if HubSpot updated a script library (where code is housed and referenced for various site functionality), our custom code was sometimes incompatible with the update, which required more custom code to "fix" the problem. Although the sites were effective, they became unwieldy, expensive, and time-consuming to build and eventually manage.

As we matured as an organization, we began to look for a better way. First, we had to better understand what the word "template" meant and overcome the stigma of using preset elements to create effective websites. Many of you reading this may hear "template" and think cookie cutter or low effort and low quality, but that truly only applies to low-value deliverables.

You can templatize high-quality outcomes without losing your competitive edge. Mercedes-Benz and Rolex are among the two most well-known luxury brands in existence, and I hate to break it to you, but that Submariner Rolex you may have your eyes on (I certainly do) wasn't built without a template, and neither was the S-Class Benz you see on the road. Even the upper echelons of luxury rely on repeatable processes via build templates to ensure quality. If you still want to characterize templates as something that precludes quality, you've got an outmoded mindset.

Think of templates as a guidepost, a result by which others should be measured and modeled. Set up templates that allow for plug and play as much as possible. A steering column in an S-Class Mercedes should fit the designed steering wheel every time. The company that machines the parts that fit the designs doesn't tear down and rebuild the tools and dies after every product; it leaves the die in place to repeat the product to have a uniform output. You need to do the same with marketing templates. Build them for scalable, repeatable, and high-quality outputs.

GUIDES

So where do guides fit into all this, and how are they different from templates?

Well, if a template dictates an output, a guide informs the template user how the template should be utilized. This is your "secret sauce." A guide documents "your way." Clear, easy-to-follow, and, ideally, step-by-step guides help ensure the templates you've created aren't open for interpretation. They are the Rosetta Stone by which all deliverables are equated.

The test of a truly well-built guide is when a complex task or outcome can be completed by someone with no to little experience in the produced outcome. If you can take a low-level employee and sit them in front of a guide that references a specific template with an example output, and at the end of the day they succeed in producing a facsimile of your desired outcome, you have a very successful guide. If you get your guides and templates to a place where a lower-salary staffer can complete the outputs usually reserved for a high-level employee, even if just for a percentage of the output and not the entire deliverable, and you're still able to charge the same fee, you've just increased the profit for your organization by servicing for the same price at a reduced cost without losing quality. Additionally, you've freed up your higher-salary employee for other efforts, which may involve better servicing high-level accounts or activities. Or you may even parlay that higher salary into a cost savings by reducing staff and rendering that role less critical to company success, as well as democratizing the work across additional employees, again freeing you from the trap of having siloed expertise reside in one chair.

LESSON LEARNED

WASTING THE TIME AWAY (AND MONEY)

As a fledgling agency, we used to do everything customized. Every strategy session, every website, and every deliverable was built from scratch. In the early

THE GREAT 8 PILLARS

days, this approach was valuable as we were still learning what worked and what didn't. Iterations of the same deliverable assisted us in building best practices.

Fast-forward several years, and routine tasks were taking far too long to maintain a profitable business. If you manage a marketing team or work on one, you must make efficient use of your team's time. Templates and guides are one of the easiest ways to do this.

As a case in point, when we began holding our marketing strategy workshops, we considered them loss-leader projects. By "loss-leader," I mean that we were losing money on each and every workshop due to complete customization of each instance. Every client email, agenda, questionnaire, and facilitated session was unique. We spent hours and hours developing the materials and deliverables. Today, these workshops are very profitable for us. We honed our approach, removed bottlenecks, and streamlined how we delivered each workshop. Emails, agendas, questionnaires, and presentation decks were templatized. We then created guides or instruction manuals for our team so that they knew how to execute.

> Don't underestimate the power of templates and guides. Templates don't equate to cheap or generic, and guides should be considered best practices.

So where do you start?

First, identify any marketing outputs or tasks that you do on a regular basis, no matter how complex they may seem. Document how it all gets done. It will likely be a messy document on your first pass, but you'll get a good general overview of how the sausage is made.

Another thing we usually see during this exercise is that you almost immediately identify efficiencies. Once you document how things are done, consider what an ideal output looks like. Revisit your archives to see a quality deliverable. You'll soon come to one of three realizations:

1. You don't like what you've found and need to rethink what you want to deliver.
2. You immediately identify a deliverable to model.
3. You have multiple outputs where you like a few things from each but no one coherent deliverable (the most common).

Regardless of which bucket you find yourself in, you need to be clear and conscious of what an ideal output looks like because it's going to become the mold from which other outputs are modeled.

Once you've documented your sequential steps (guide) in achieving your model output, then strip away from that final deliverable any items that need to be added and uncovered during your engagement of the guide. For example, if you consistently produce weekly or monthly marketing reports within PowerPoint, leave the tables, graphs, text areas, and any other entry points, but remove the data or add placeholder-only elements. This then becomes the template you'll use to create future deliverables.

Templates and guides only work if they are universal to the output. What I mean is it's easy to fall down the slippery slope of everyone tweaking the guide and template "just a little" and then utilizing that tweaked version as their new template and how-to guide. These documents tend to take on a life of their own at that point, and you no longer have "your way of doing things." Instead, you have multiple ways of doing things, which means there is no central "truth" to your outputs. You'll quickly see quality and efficiency go out the window; additionally, you'll have again siloed information and production into only a few seats, and should that institutional knowledge leave, you're left back at square one.

That isn't to say that templates, guides, and even model deliverables won't change. In fact, they will and should adjust as better and better ways to service and deliver are uncovered. However, this should be a conscious and centralized effort that is managed by a single owner or, at the very least, a unified oversight committee whose job is to ensure standardization of efforts and coordination of changes should efficiencies be identified.

A quick internet search will deliver just about any template or guide you can imagine. Today, you can find templates and guides for every aspect of marketing, including full-blown website templates. My experience is that these templates and guides can be extremely valuable, saving your company time and money. However, it is wise to test them out and do your research. Not all resources are created equal; making the wrong choice can end up costing you more than you save.

GOLD STANDARDS

Does your marketing team require new or updated templates? Consider the following questions to help you decide:

1. Does your marketing team leverage templates and guides to improve productivity?
2. Does your website incorporate standardized templates for landing pages, form pages, and primary content pages?
3. Does your marketing operation leverage standardized templates for case studies, sell sheets, and standardized marketing collateral?
4. Do you leverage standardized templates for reporting?

There are many forms of templates and guides that you can incorporate into your marketing operations. If you answered no to any of these questions, we highly recommend you start to build out templates and guides for your most critical or most often used marketing tools. These templates and guides will add hours to your day and help you to drive much stronger results!

CONCLUSION

If you are interested in driving real, measurable results for your company's marketing efforts, the time is now. Don't let old-school marketing philosophies get in the way. You now have the knowledge and tools to help you drive a 10X return on your marketing investment.

The Great 8 Pillars of ROI-Driven Marketing is a framework that I know works. I have seen it deliver amazing results time and time again. Now that you have read this book, it will help to circle back to each chapter and determine where your best effort should be focused.

- **Pillar 1: Goals, KPIs, and Industry Benchmarks— Defining Your 10X.** How to define your 10X return on marketing investment, create SMART goals, and determine what to track

- **Pillar 2: Value Proposition, Messaging, and Branding.** How to develop a killer value proposition

- **Pillar 3: Marketing Strategy.** How to build a marketing strategy geared for ROI

- **Pillar 4: Marketing Team Structure.** How to build the proper team structure

- **Pillar 5: Website.** How your website fits into the ROI equation

- **Pillar 6: Analytics and Reporting**. How to set up reports executives love

- **Pillar 7: Technology Stack**. Tools and software required for success

- **Pillar 8: Templates and Guides**. Key assets to increase productivity

So what do you do next? First, just get started. My gut feeling is that one or more of the chapters in this book really stood out to you. Something piqued your interest or really hit home. Begin there.

Second, go back to the end of each chapter and review the gold standards. These questions will help you prioritize your next steps.

Third, visit our website, *www.G8P.co*, to download all our free tools, guides, and templates. These resources have been optimized for marketing a manufacturing company and incorporate years of knowledge.

If you are like most marketers, you are likely struggling with the stress and constant monotony of more, more, more. You are sick and tired of wasting time on marketing that does not move the needle. You are tired of being in reaction mode every time a salesperson needs a new presentation deck or when leadership needs more business cards. You are tired of being a servant and want to be seen as a strategic leader. I know how you feel; I used to be in your shoes.

Almost every marketer I have met yearns to be relevant and make a difference. They want a seat at the table when it comes to helping their company scale. If you are done with being status quo, it's time to try something new.

It's time to take the lead on the direction of your company's marketing. It's time to set up a marketing operational infrastructure that drives real results. Imagine what your role would look like if you were delivering a 10X return on marketing investment. What would that do for your company, your team, and your career? Take that first step and begin making a difference today.

APPENDIX

Learning from the failures of others is a surefire way to fast-track your own success. That's why we've included a few more of our mistakes—and what we learned from them. Take from them what you will and, whatever you do, keep learning, growing, and moving forward.

YOU CAN'T PLEASE EVERYONE

Several years ago, we were building a new website for a manufacturing company. The client's existing website was a disaster. It was old, broken, and filled with errors. It did not meet any of the qualities and standards we have discussed herein. To be honest, we should have recommended taking it down and putting up a temporary one-page placeholder until the new site launched. However, it had been up for several years and had probably done its damage.

We built the client a new website and received client approvals at every step of the process. The president was very happy with the product and couldn't wait to get it launched. Then something happened. The president of the company, the person we worked with throughout the process, the person who signed off on everything, didn't want to launch the new site. He stated he didn't like the editorial copy on the home page. This came as a surprise, as he had already reviewed and approved it. Regardless, we solicited his feedback and reworked the copy. He approved it again, and we uploaded it to the site, but guess what: he still didn't want to launch.

At this point, he had paid 100 percent for the website, and it was 100 percent complete. He had paid over $50,000 for the site and all of the supporting assets and then never launched the site. It was one of the strangest situations I have been a part of in marketing. The only thing I can think is that perhaps there was another issue or opportunity that he didn't want to tell us about, something outside of our control.

Years later, he launched a new site with another agency. However, this project still haunts me. I wish I had been able to rectify his concerns. I think if we had written this book earlier, we would have been able to use it to guide him through the effectiveness of the website strategy and editorial content.

LESSON LEARNED

DON'T LET SALESPEOPLE STAND IN THE WAY

My experience is that most companies' sales and marketing departments are completely separate. They rarely talk to each other, and if they do, it is because sales needs something. By aligning with sales leadership, you are beginning to pave the way for mutual success and teamwork. Don't be put off if individual salespeople are hesitant to work with you. They often like to be lone wolves, chasing prey and taking credit for their hard work. They have never experienced a marketing team that hands them warm leads. If you find this to be the case, don't be offended. Just stick with it. If you follow the chapters in this book, you will have the strategy, rigor, processes, systems, and tools to track your success and prove that what you do matters.

We had been working with an electronics manufacturing company for five years and had built a great relationship with their leadership team. We were actively tracking leads and ROI metrics via HubSpot Marketing Hub. The company needed to invest further in sales and marketing, as competition was stealing market share.

The owner (let's call him Jeff) decided to hire a new VP of sales and invest in a new customer relationship management system. We were super excited, as they really needed a formal system to close the loop on ROI tracking and closed customers.

Fast-forward a couple of months, and "Rick" was hired as the VP of sales. Rick was not from the manufacturing industry and had a very specific plan for sales growth. He challenged everything we had been doing and wanted to shift gears. He did not believe in online marketing and wanted to invest in television commercials (because there is such a strong precedent for selling manufacturing widgets to the general public; yes, I was snarky about it).

Anyway, Rick was not drinking the marketing juice. He was doing his best to make us irrelevant. Shortly thereafter, we were analyzing sales reports and noticed that Rick was working on a $100,000 opportunity with a new client, which he eventually won. We were excited since it was a marketing-generated lead.

As you can imagine, Rick took all the credit and said marketing was not a factor in the sale. He stated to his leadership team, "I've been working that lead for months, and while the prospect may have visited the website, it was because I sent them there."

Little did Rick know, we were able to track this opportunity all the way back to the prospect's first point of contact with our client, which had been years before Rick's arrival at the company. We were able to prove that the prospect engaged with the marketing materials we had sent over the years as well. To put some icing on the cake, we were able to pull up the website form that the prospect filled out just weeks earlier, asking to be contacted by a sales team member. So I asked Rick, "If you have been working this lead for months, why didn't they just call you or email you directly? Why did they go through the trouble of filling out a form on the website and asking to be contacted by a sales representative?"

Rick didn't last long at that company.

I tell this story not to diminish Rick but to illustrate how salespeople can be a roadblock to team success. The objective is for the organization to reach its goals, and it takes a team to get there.

LESSON LEARNED

CONVERSION RATE CONVERTS

Years ago, we had the opportunity to consult for a client that had an e-commerce website. The company had a successful brick-and-mortar business with eight locations throughout the Midwest. Unfortunately, their e-commerce website was in bad shape. When I say bad shape, I mean really bad. The website was only getting about $5,000 of sales per month, which equated to approximately fifty sales per month at an average order value of $100.

We were hired to consult on how to improve the website's ROI. Upon completing our analysis, we found that the website was getting approximately 20,000 visitors per month. With only fifty sales transactions per month, this equated to a 0.0025 percent visitor-to-sale conversion rate—absolutely horrible.

After further research, we were able to determine that much of their traffic consisted of high-quality ideal customer profiles and buyers. We were able to use this knowledge to further identify the key issues affecting sales and focused on the website itself. We found a plethora of issues on the website, including missing product information, security issues, and the inability to check out in certain browsers.

With this additional knowledge, we informed the client that the resolution to their problems was quite simple. Fix the site and their sales would significantly improve. We were able to model a $40,000–$60,000 sales increase per month just by fixing the issues and improving the conversion rate, a 12X multiplier.

Conversion rate optimization is something that you should never underestimate.

ACKNOWLEDGMENTS

When I started to write this book, I was admittedly overwhelmed. I had never written a book before, and the idea of putting my ideas on paper for the world to read added a level of vulnerability I was not sure I was ready for. Would readers like my book? Would anyone care about its contents? This book would have never been written without the encouragement of several people.

First and foremost, I would like to thank my wife, Jane. To describe Jane as incredible is an understatement. If it were not for Jane's support, guidance, and patience, I would have never started my company, and this book would not have been possible. Thank you for all that you do. I am lucky to have you in my life.

I would also like to thank two key contributors to this book.

Nadine Nocero-Tye and I have worked together for over ten years. Nadine is not just an expert in B2B marketing but also is a loyal friend and an incredible person. She wrote several chapters of this book and added insights to many others. Nadine also helped me develop many of the methodologies outlined in this book. Nadine, I can't thank you enough.

John Daters was the impetus for the writing of this book. You can read more about John and how this book came to be in Chapter 5: The Great 8 Pillars of ROI-Driven Marketing. John helped me see that we had something worthy of writing about. He also wrote two of the chapters of this book. John's background is rooted in search engine optimization, but his true north is managing people. John, thank you for all that you do every day.

I would also like to thank all of the employees and clients of SyncShow (my marketing agency), both past and present. Every one of you provided a challenge, insight, idea, or best practice that helped us to build our methodologies. I am indebted to you all. I have had the pleasure of working with so many great marketers and companies in my career and wouldn't change it for the world.

Last but not least, I would like to thank Joey Gilkey from Sales Driven Agency. Joey introduced me to new ways of thinking about sales and how people make buying decisions. If you are looking to improve your sales process, Joey and his team are fantastic.

ABOUT THE AUTHORS

Chris Peer, Nadine Nocero-Tye, and John Daters collectively bring over fifty years of B2B marketing experience. Our knowledge gained and "lessons learned" have helped build the methodologies outlined in this book. All three of us work together at SyncShow, a boutique marketing agency focused on driving a 10X return on investment for our clients.

It is with special thanks and gratitude that we have had the opportunity to work with some of the most amazing manufacturing companies. Without them, we could not have written this book. We also are grateful to all the companies that were inspirational for our Lesson Learned sections placed throughout the book. While we strive to avoid mistakes, they sometimes happen. When they do, we learn from them and become stronger.

CPSIA information can be obtained
at www.ICGtesting.com
Printed in the USA
JSHW020048060723
43828JS00001B/1/J